Photograph of the children making their First Holy Communion in 1935 in the parish church of Aschau am Inn. (*Joseph Ratzinger is in the red circle.*)

Pope Benedict XVI

Servant of the Truth

EDITED BY PETER SEEWALD

Translated by Brian McNeil, C.R.V.

IGNATIUS PRESS   SAN FRANCISCO

Title of the German original:
Der deutsche Papst: von Joseph Ratzinger zu Benedikt XVI.
© 2005 Peter Seewald
© 2005 Verlagsgruppe Weltbild GmbH, Steinerne Furt 67, 86167 Augsburg
and Axel Springer AG, Axel-Springer-Platz 1, 20350 Hamburg, Germany

Front cover photograph:
Pope Benedict XVI greets the world from
the central balcony of St. Peter's Basilica,
April 19, 2005.
By
Giancarlo Giuliani/CPP

Front cover design by Roxanne Mei Lum

Back cover photograph credits:

Upper left:	*Corbis/Allesandro Bianchi*	Middle right: *Corbis/Tony Gentile*
Upper middle:	*Corbis*	Lower right: *DPB/epa/Tony Gentile/Pool*
Upper right:	*Getty Images/HO*	Middle left: *Corbis/Stringer*

Back cover design by John Herreid

© 2006 by Ignatius Press, San Francisco
All rights reserved
ISBN 978-1-58617-151-3
ISBN 1-58617-151-8
Library of Congress Control Number 2006923031
Printed in Canada ∞

Contents

Foreword, *by Kai Diekmann*   5

Peter Seewald
Introduction   35
Born on Holy Saturday   36
Ratzinger in the Hitler Youth   44
Liberation and a New Start   46
My Brother the Pope   50
A Life for God   56

Elmar Gruber
He Showed Us the Way to God's Love   64

Peter Seewald
Co-Workers of the Truth   68
Il tedesco—A German in Rome   84
The Handmaid of God   96

Hans-Jochen Jaschke
He Brings Us the Spirit of Joy in the Faith   102

Peter Seewald
Friends of God   106
Habemus papam!   110

Joseph Cardinal Ratzinger
Against the Dictatorship of Relativism   122

Peter Seewald
How the New Pope Will Change the World   132

Pope Benedict XVI
I Am Not Alone!   152

Peter Seewald
Pontiff of Love   158
"God's Revolution": The World Youth Day in Cologne   168

Biography   184

Bibliography   186

Photographs   188

Foreword

Kai Diekmann,
chief editor of *Bild* newspaper.

Roughly one year has passed since the conclave elected the German Cardinal Joseph Ratzinger as the successor of Peter. It is too early to say how things will develop, but one thing is already clear: Benedict XVI is resolved to continue the inheritance of his predecessor. Like the great John Paul II, he too is a "pope of people's hearts", who seeks the encounter with the faithful.

Very few would have expected that. Many saw the new Pope as the spokesman of a harsh, dogmatically rigid faith, with an absoluteness about it that had little interest in the reality and the distress of humanity.

Nothing could be farther from the truth! The visible joy of the Pope when he met young people at the World Youth Day in Cologne in 2005 was already a sign of the serene humanity of this pontificate. With his first encyclical—which is traditionally understood as a kind of "program of government" by the Vicar of Christ— Benedict XVI continued this line. Its title is: *Deus caritas est*, "God is love." The central motif of the words of this Pope is neither progress nor the collapse in values: rather, Benedict XVI chooses the very heart of the Christian message, human love as an expression of God's providential love, and love as the criterion of our action, as the only valid foundation for our life. This is an astonishing and courageous starting point, especially today. But it perfectly fits the modest and kindly character of the Pope from Bavaria, whose true nature and intentions have so often been misunderstood.

The journalist Peter Seewald has an intimate knowledge both of the Vatican and of the Church in Germany, and he has accompanied the Pope for many years. This makes him uniquely suited to portray this pontificate of love— which is the goal of Benedict XVI.

Kai Diekmann

The face of faith

A portrait of Joseph Ratzinger taken in 1999. One of the most powerful men in the Vatican, he fights on behalf of truth and faith: "A society from which God is absent destroys itself."

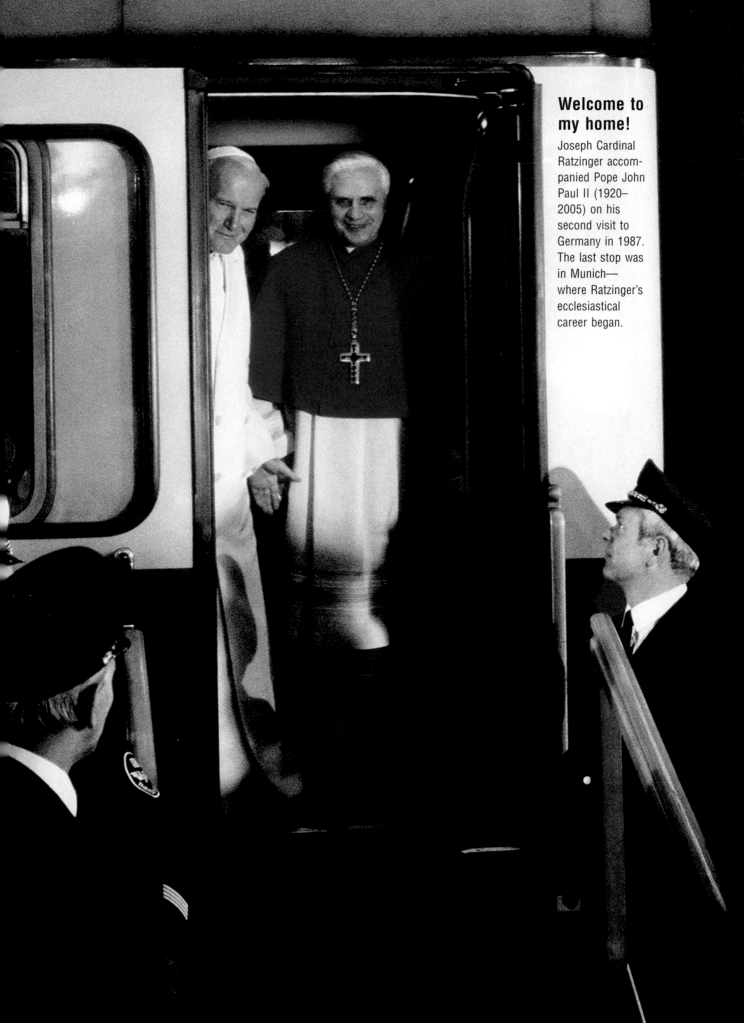

Welcome to my home!

Joseph Cardinal Ratzinger accompanied Pope John Paul II (1920–2005) on his second visit to Germany in 1987. The last stop was in Munich—where Ratzinger's ecclesiastical career began.

Goodbye, Munich!

After five years as Archbishop of Munich and Freising, Joseph Ratzinger said farewell on the Marienplatz in Munich: Pope John Paul II had called him to head the Congregation for the Doctrine of the Faith in Rome.

A blessing for the whole world

A joyful and enthusiastic welcome for Benedict XVI. Half a million faithful completely fill Saint Peter's Square, and the Pope makes his way through the crowd in his "popemobile".

In his garden at home

The photograph (1989) shows Joseph Cardinal Ratzinger with his sister, Maria (1922–1991), in the garden of his house in Pentling near Regensburg. He bought the house in 1967—intending to spend his retirement there.

Greetings from his home country
A guard of honor of the Bavarian Mountain Guard salutes Joseph Cardinal Ratzinger in Rome in April 2002, bringing greetings from his home country on his seventy-fifth birthday.

Two servants of God

September 11, 2002: Joseph Cardinal Ratzinger assists John Paul II (1920–2005) at the memorial Mass in Saint Peter's in Rome for the victims of the terrorist attacks in New York. In his homily, the Pope said: "Only love can overcome hatred."

Bidding farewell to John Paul II

At the close of the funeral Mass in Saint Peter's Square, Joseph Cardinal Ratzinger blesses the coffin of John Paul II. The Book of the Gospels lies on the coffin.

The first blessing "urbi et orbi"

6:49 P.M. on April 19, 2005: Benedict XVI after the proclamation of his election. "I entrust myself", he said, "to the prayers of the faithful." The cardinals, too, paid homage to the new Pope.

"We Are Pope!"

The headline "*Wir sind Papst!*" appeared in the *Bild*, expressing pride at the election of Benedict XVI. Here we see him traveling across Saint Peter's Square for the first time. The crowds cheer—and many Germans are there, too, waving their flags.

Brothers by blood

They take one step closer to their Creator by consecrating their lives to the Lord. In June 1951, Joseph Ratzinger (24, *right*) and his older brother, Georg (27, *left*), are ordained to the priesthood in Freising. With outstretched hands they impart their first blessing.

Habemus papam!
April 19, 2005: The first
German pope for 482 years
presents himself to the
faithful on the loggia of
Saint Peter's basilica.

The Cardinal and the angel

Their common language was prayer. Joseph Cardinal Ratzinger and Mother Teresa shared, not always the same way of doing things, but always the same belief: "Mankind must be led to God in love."

The Cardinal and the children

A father in faith: Cardinal Ratzinger fights to protect the earthly family that he himself never had. "A direct desire for a family of my own? My plans never went that far."

Teacher of Sacred Scripture

During his inaugural Mass, Benedict XVI holds the text of Sacred Scripture. "Do not be afraid of Christ!" The new Pope shows the world the One whom he follows.

Ritual of humility

"If I do not wash you, you have no share in me" (Jn 13). As Jesus washed the feet of his disciples, so Joseph Ratzinger washes the feet of Catholic priests in the Vatican. Sacred Scripture comes alive in what he does here.

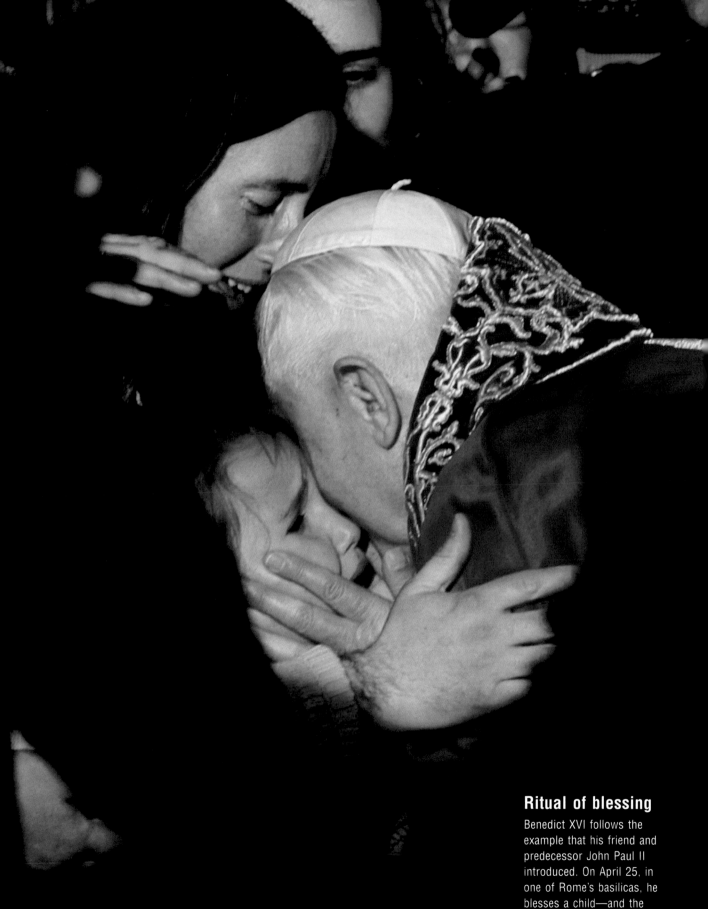

Ritual of blessing

Benedict XVI follows the example that his friend and predecessor John Paul II introduced. On April 25, in one of Rome's basilicas, he blesses a child—and the faithful stretch out their hands to touch him.

Guardian of doctrinal purity

The long path to the true faith. Cardinal Ratzinger in the colonnade of 248 pillars that encompasses Saint Peter's Square. As Prefect of the Congregation for the Doctrine of the Faith, he spoke with the bishops of every continent. His working day lasted sixteen hours. Now, it is not likely to be any shorter.

Representative of God on earth

Habemus papam ex Germania! There are around 400,000 people in Saint Peter's Square, and the German flags are waving. On the balcony, the new Pope Benedict XVI smiles gently. He is the first German on the throne of Peter for 482 years, a "humble worker in the vineyard of the Lord". His gaze is directed ahead.

It is in the Cross that he finds support; the Cross is his future: "Do not be afraid of Christ. He takes nothing away, and he gives you everything." "The Church is young. She holds within herself the future of the world", said Pope Benedict XVI in his homily in the solemn inaugural Mass in Saint Peter's Square. Saint Peter is said to have given his disciples a shepherd's staff when he sent them out on a missionary journey.

Introduction

Peter Seewald,
editor of this book.

It all began in Rome, in November 1992. I was sitting on one of the red Baroque chairs in the audience room of the Congregation for the Doctrine of the Faith, when the door opened and a delicate man with fine features entered. We sat down at the window and talked about him, about his work, and about God. This was the beginning of a process that was to change my life.

Once, we drove at top speed through the Vatican in his secretary's new Golf. The high dignitary in the passenger's seat sang like Pavarotti (well, almost like Pavarotti). On our way to Montecassino, the monastery of Saint Benedict, we stopped to eat at a restaurant. He took his place with his tray in the queue and then said grace—like any rural parish priest. I was impressed by his supreme personal ease, by his Bavarian heart, by the breadth of his thinking.

There is no one who can listen with such concentration—and reply with such precision. In the course of our interviews, he sometimes flung his foot over the arm of his chair like a young, inquisitive student. And when he spoke of the ordering of the universe, one could sense something of the God who holds this world together.

Joseph Ratzinger is a spiritual master and a great teacher of the Church. He taught me what it meant to swim against the stream. "The Church needs a revolution of faith!" he cried. When our society began to drift off into a situation of spiritual negligence where "anything goes", he became one of the harshest critics of "modern living". He explained his passionate intensity by saying that Christ demands a radical exodus. The great element of continuity in his life is the desire to preserve the faith of the fathers for their grandchildren. Some people call this conservative. I have come more and more to see it as something absolutely essential.

A new age of faith began with John Paul II. With his successor, the "new spring of the human spirit" of which Karol Wojtyla spoke is now becoming perceptible. The crisis of religion will not be overcome at a single stroke, but this Pope is looking for the keys precisely where they were lost. He wants to lead the Church back to her roots, to Christ himself.

Benedict XVI, the "blessed" man, will thus not only renew the Church and become in his own turn a patron of Europe; he will also change Germany, that country which has played such an important role for the whole of Christendom. This means that we must come to know the message of Jesus anew. It contains immense treasures that we have failed to see!

Peter Seewald
Editor

35

Born on Holy Saturday

Sometimes it seems as if some people receive their vocation while still in the cradle, and the goal of their entire life is to fulfill this vocation—that, at any rate, is true of Pope Benedict XVI.

Joseph Aloysius Ratzinger was born at 4:15 one frosty morning, when the little town of Marktl am Inn was covered in snow and ice. His parents were called Maria and Joseph. And since April 16, 1927, was Holy Saturday, the little boy was baptized very soon after his birth: he was the first to be christened in the newly blessed water, receiving a literal immersion into the mystery of Easter. Liturgically speaking, Holy Saturday is the hour of the Church's birth, and it was not only his parents and relatives who saw the circumstances of Joseph's birth as the sign of a particular grace from God. Joseph Ratzinger himself has said that the beginning of his life, "on the very threshold of Easter, which had not yet come", has always filled him with gratitude: "For that could only be a sign of God's blessing."

Marktl am Inn lies on the border between Lower and Upper Bavaria in the ancient diocese of Passau, close to Altötting, a center of Marian pilgrimages where Saint Conrad of Parzham ("The Cross is my book") was the porter in the Capuchin monastery.

His parents married late. His father, Joseph, was a Bavarian policeman with the rank of commissioner. He came from the Bavarian Forest and looked after geese on the farm where he was born. He was a rational, just, and strict man—perhaps too strict. "But" (as his son writes) "we always sensed that it was his kindness that led him to be strict. He did not think in the way that people [under Nazism] were supposed to think at that time, and he did so with a sovereign self-awareness that was utterly convincing." Above all, his judgments were always "astonishingly accurate".

His mother, Maria, had trained as a cook. She was the daughter of a baker in Southern Tyrol, and her "warm-heartedness" made up for much of her husband's strictness. She could turn her hand to everything. She sewed their own clothes, she made soap, and even in times when there was not much food she "could somehow make a good meal out of a few very simple ingredients". With her three children—Maria was five years older and Georg three years older than Joseph, the youngest—she went on pilgrimage to sanctuaries such as the Ponlach chapel at the waterfall in the wood, and on their way home they plucked wild "lamb's lettuce". When the children attended grade school, they had to pay a fee for their education, since they refused to join the Hitler Youth (although they were later compelled to do so). She earned the money by seasonal work on farms in Reit im Winkel. She saved wherever possible and lived simply: she never spent more than she had to and made a prudent use of her resources, completely in keeping with the Rule of Saint Benedict. Her children said that this spirit of renunciation generated "an inner solidarity" in the family and also meant that they could take pleasure "even in the smallest things".

Ready for the ABCs of life: Joseph Ratzinger in his first class in the primary school in Aschau am Inn, 1932. His family moved to this little town on the border between Germany and Austria on December 5, when his father was appointed policeman there.

The family of Pope Benedict XVI in the mid-1930s: father Joseph, daughter Maria, mother Maria, and sons Georg and Joseph (*from right to left*).

Maria and Joseph—His Parents

Maria Ratzinger (died December 16, 1963) came from Mühlbach in the Puster Valley in South Tyrol. She was the daughter of a baker and had trained as a cook. Her family was so poor that some of her sisters emigrated to America. Joseph Ratzinger, the Pope's father (died August 23, 1959), came from Lower Bavaria. After serving as a soldier, he became a policeman in the Bavarian Rural Police Force. Their daughter, Maria, was born in 1922, their son Georg in 1924, and Joseph in 1927. Two years after Joseph's birth, the family moved from Marktl am Inn to Tittmoning, then to Aschau. In 1933, the father bought a farm in Hufschlag near Traunstein. Joseph Ratzinger describes his father as "a just but strict man". He says of his mother: "Her warm-heartedness" compensated for "what may have been excessive strictness" in his father. In order to pay for the education of her children, she took seasonal work on farms. Ratzinger writes: "She had to do without so many things. This led to a profound inner solidarity with us children."

Grace before meals, evening prayers, regular churchgoing: religion was a basic theme of their family life. The father, who was a great educator, explained the Gospel to his children from a handbook for the laity, and he gave them books, which Joseph eagerly read as an introduction "to the mysterious world of the liturgy". Later on, he was to remember with particular fondness the early morning Masses in the cold and snowy winter days before Christmas, when the church was lit only by candles; he recalled the devotions to Christ in Gethsemane and the celebration of the Resurrection. The whole church was in darkness, but when the priest announced: "Christ is risen!"—"all the curtains fell to the ground at once, and the church was flooded with light." They were able to "experience liturgy as a feast".

Commissioner Ratzinger was frequently moved from one post to another. Two years after Joseph's birth, they moved from Marktl to Tittmoning, then from Tittmoning to Aschau. In the villages where he worked as policeman, he regularly patrolled his beat, and his son recalls: "This had the advantage that he knew everybody. If a crime was committed, he knew whom to suspect!" The Baroque burgh of Tittmoning, with its proud townhouses, the majestic city square, the little castle on a hill, and the monastery church, became for Joseph "my childhood's land of dreams".

In Aschau, the Ratzingers lived on the upper floor of a farmer's villa, and Joseph once

The house in which Pope Benedict XVI was born in Marktl am Inn at 4:15 A.M. on Holy Saturday, April 16, 1927. He was baptized only four hours later.

nearly drowned in the garden pond. On the ground floor lived the assistant constable, who went out early each morning with his wife to take part in military sports: he was a convinced Nazi and noted down what was said in the sermons in church. Joseph was an altar boy and once saw his parish priest being beaten up by Hitler's followers. His father refused to join any Nazi organization. On Sundays, he smoked a Virginia cigar as he read the *Right Path*, an anti-fascist newspaper to which he had a subscription. He often fell into a rage at the disgraceful actions of the Nazis. Joseph learned how to argue his case: "Everyone knew that I went to church, or even that I wanted to become a priest. This meant that I became involved in debates, and I had to learn what weapons I could use."

On the day Hitler came to power, his father announced: "Now there will be war. Now we need a house." In the same year, 1933, he bought for the sum of about 3,350 dollars a house, originally built in 1726 but now seriously dilapidated, near Traunstein; the family moved in four years later. There was no running water, only a well with a pump. The farmhouse had an idyllic location at the edge of the woods, with a view of the mountains. The children enjoyed the old barns where one could not only "dream glorious dreams" but also smoke in secret. Franz Niegel, who was at school with Joseph, says: "It was never depressing to visit the Ratzingers. His parents were very warmhearted, as in the good old days. They were modest and simple. As a student, Joseph was never one of those who were unpleasantly pious. He was always normal. He just wanted to be a believing and good Christian."

Their inclinations were obvious at an early age. Georg declared that he wanted to be music director in the cathedral. Joseph was undecided—first, he was impressed by a house painter, then he wanted to be a bricklayer. But one day, Cardinal Faulhaber arrived from Munich, a prince of the Church in his scarlet robes, and Joseph knew: "That's what I

Non scholae, sed vitae discimus— we learn, not for the school, but for life itself! Joseph Ratzinger (*circle*) in the classroom of the primary school in Aschau am Inn.

The schoolhouse in Aschau am Inn, where Joseph Ratzinger attended school from 1932 to 1937. His parents gave him a missal as early as his second year!

nearly drowned in the garden pond. On the ground floor lived the assistant constable, who went out early each morning with his wife to take part in military sports: he was a convinced Nazi and noted down what was said in the sermons in church. Joseph was an altar boy and once saw his parish priest being beaten up by Hitler's followers. His father refused to join any Nazi organization. On Sundays, he smoked a Virginia cigar as he read the *Right Path*, an anti-fascist newspaper to which he had a subscription. He often fell into a rage at the disgraceful actions of the Nazis. Joseph learned how to argue his case: "Everyone knew that I went to church, or even that I wanted to become a priest. This meant that I became involved in debates, and I had to learn what weapons I could use."

On the day Hitler came to power, his father announced: "Now there will be war. Now we need a house." In the same year, 1933, he bought for the sum of about 3,350 dollars a house, originally built in 1726 but now seriously dilapidated, near Traunstein; the family moved in four years later. There was no running water, only a well with a pump. The farmhouse had an idyllic location at the edge of the woods, with a view of the mountains. The children enjoyed the old barns where one could not only "dream glorious dreams" but also smoke in secret. Franz Niegel, who was at school with Joseph, says: "It was never depressing to visit the Ratzingers. His parents were very warm-hearted, as in the good old days. They were modest and simple.

As a student, Joseph was never one of those who were unpleasantly pious. He was always normal. He just wanted to be a believing and good Christian."

Their inclinations were obvious at an early age. Georg declared that he wanted to be music director in the cathedral. Joseph was undecided—first, he was impressed by a house painter, then he wanted to be a bricklayer.

want to be too!" At home, the brothers sometimes played at being priests ... but once, during a procession with candles, the two brothers burned their sister's braids ...

Maria attended the secondary school run by the Franciscan Sisters, and Georg entered the diocesan minor seminary in Traunstein. As the youngest child, Joseph went everywhere with his father, who was now a pensioner, and he enjoyed this time: "Walking and telling stories, we became very close." However, the village priest insisted that Joseph ought to go to the seminary, in order to learn the spiritual life in a systematic way. This was a shock for the child. He felt that all the breath was knocked out of him when he sat in a classroom with about sixty other boys, and he had only one word for physical education in the playground: "torture".

The brown plague of Nazism penetrated their high school, too, but there were some who displayed a firm attitude. One music teacher told the boys to omit the words "Death to Judah!" (*Juda den Tod*) in their songbook and to sing instead: "Reverse our distress!" (*Wende die Not*).

Joseph was at the top of his class, but he was never unpopular, since he let his classmates copy his homework. He "read Goethe with great delight, but I found Schiller a little too moralizing." He wrote poems about daily life and nature and helped others with their studies. His fellow pupil Ludwig Wihr recalls: "He was a superman even then, especially in Latin and Greek; a quiet pupil, but not a coward in any way." Georg relates that even at the age of ten, his brother had a daily plan that he followed exactly: "After the meal, he rested a little, lying on the sofa. Then

"He wrote poems about daily life and nature and helped others with their studies"

he did his homework. He always observed the motto: 'Duty comes first!'"

In 1943, the Traunstein seminarians were enlisted for work in the anti-aircraft batteries in Munich. Ratzinger was sixteen when he saw the city collapse bit by bit into ruins. He worked first in the anti-aircraft measurements department and later in the telephone exchange at Gilching on Ammer Lake. In the meantime, the students took an abbreviated high school examination at the Maximilian High School in Munich. In the fall of 1944, the young men were sent off for two months to the border between Austria and Hungary. First they drilled with their spades, then they dug with them. A vast host of forced laborers from every corner of Europe was to build a "south-eastern wall" as quickly as possible. "However, we never learned how to shoot—and in any case, our weapons were not loaded."

In the chaos of Hitler's "final struggle", Joseph's troop was transferred back to the barracks at home, and the boys had "to march through Traunstein singing songs about the war". Ratzinger was taken prisoner by the Americans. An endless procession of the defeated wound its way on foot along the highway, with their final destination a huge camp in a field near Ulm. Fifty thousand men hung around in the open air, no matter what the weather; their rations were one spoonful of soup and one piece of bread each day. Joseph was released on June 19, 1945. When he arrived home on June 22 and heard people praying and singing at the evening service in the church in Traunstein, he was exuberantly happy. "Not even the heavenly Jerusalem would have seemed lovelier to me at that particular moment."

The interior of Saint Oswald's church in Marktl am Inn, where Joseph was baptized.

Birth certificate of Joseph Aloysius Ratzinger, issued by the registrar in Marktl am Inn.

The three-hundred-year-old registry of births in the town where Benedict XVI was born.

43

Ratzinger in the Hitler Youth

It made the headlines throughout the world: sixty years after the war, a German was elected Pope by a clear majority of the 115 cardinals (including Ratzinger) who were in the conclave. The world celebrated Benedict XVI from Bavaria—but in some countries, he was linked to the Nazi period.

"From Hitler Youth to Papa Ratzi", proclaimed the *Sun* in London, and the *Standard* in Brussels called him "the panzer cardinal".

Editor Peter Seewald asked Cardinal Ratzinger in 1996: "Were you in the Hitler Youth?"

Ratzinger replied: "To begin with, we [that is, he and his brother, Georg] were not members. But when a general obligation to join was introduced, my brother was dutifully enrolled. I was still too young, but later, when I was in the minor seminary, I was enlisted in the Hitler Youth. As soon as I left the seminary, I stopped attending the meetings." His refusal to attend these meetings had grave financial consequences. In order to get a reduction in the school fees for Joseph—a reduction that the family really needed—it was necessary to produce evidence that the boy had attended the Hitler Youth meetings. However, a teacher saved the day: "Thanks be to God, there was a very understanding mathematics teacher. He was himself a Nazi, but he was an honest man, and he said to me: 'I understand you, I'll see that things are settled.' And so I was able to avoid the meetings."

At the age of sixteen, Ratzinger became an anti-aircraft auxiliary, something that was terrible "especially for as unmilitary a person as I am". His unit protected a BMW automobile factory near Munich, and then he was moved to the anti-aircraft measurements department and to the central telephone exchange in Gilching on Ammer Lake. He deserted in the last days of the war. That could have cost him his life: deserters were shot on the spot by the SS.

But Ratzinger survived. He was stopped by two German soldiers near Traunstein, and although they guessed that he was deserting, they let him go. He was lucky a second time also: when he came home, two SS men were billeted with his parents. The Nazis were suspicious when they saw the young man, since he was clearly old enough to be fighting, and they wanted to take him with them for cross-examination. But his father raged and screamed until the SS men desisted and went away.

Equating membership in the Hitler Youth with being a Nazi is a harsh accusation that infuriates many others of the Pope's generation.

In *Der Untergang*, Joachim Fest, historian and biographer of Hitler, says: "Such absurd accusations can be explained only on the basis of ignorance. In 1939, membership was made obligatory for all children, and no one could evade it. The Hitler Youth were children, not criminals!" Ratzinger and the Hitler Youth—a German story. Franz Schirrmacher, editor of the *FAZ* newspaper, writes: "Unlike his immediate predecessor, Ratzinger was not born on the morally intact side of the planet. This makes him—in a wholly unpatriotic sense—one of us."

Joseph Ratzinger, aged sixteen, as an auxiliary air-raid helper. He joined an anti-aircraft battery near Munich but later deserted.

Liberation and a New Start

The Second World War ended on May 8, 1945: Nazi Germany was defeated. Joseph Ratzinger was just eighteen years old, and for him, the day of liberation came to symbolize a new start.

In an interview with the *FAZ* newspaper, he recalled: "Germany lay in ruins, and we had to start all over again both in the material and in the intellectual sphere. Our country was internationally isolated and despised—so how could we succeed in reconstructing it? And when would we be freed from the prisoner-of-war camps? Nevertheless, hope was stronger than all these worries. I had a very optimistic view of the Western Allies, and I was convinced that they were acting out of a high humane and Christian ethos and that now, after the defeat of National Socialism, we would not have to wait too long: the future would stand open before us. In a way, the state of imprisonment took on a symbolic character for me: we had no homes, we were still not free, and the nights were cold. But the days were bright and getting longer. We were going toward a better future."

On June 19, 1945, Ratzinger was released from captivity. In the spring of 1946, he began his studies at the Philosophical and Theological Academy in Freising near Munich. In his memoirs, Pope Benedict XVI writes: "The

"The men had come back from the war, and they were now full of intellectual and literary hunger"

atmosphere in the seminary was very much alive. The men had come back from the war, and they were now really full of intellectual and literary hunger. There was already a tremendous intellectual upsurge into which we were caught up."

The first book he read was *The Revolution in Thinking*, by the Munich professor of moral theology Theodor Steinbüchel (1888–1949). Joseph Ratzinger writes: "Reading this was a key experience for me." The title of the book became his own motto: for a new Germany, for a better and God-fearing world. "There was an awareness and a hope that a new epoch of Christianity was now possible."

He also read Fyodor Dostoyevsky (1821–1881) and reflected on his famous novel *Crime and Punishment*. How was the catastrophe of the Holocaust possible on Christian soil? In *Salt of the Earth*, Ratzinger replies: "Even if the SS was a criminal organization of atheists, they had nevertheless been baptized. Christian anti-Semitism had to a certain extent prepared the ground—one cannot deny this."

Crime and Punishment, The Revolution in Thinking . . . sixty years after the end of the war, a German Pope is leading the Catholic Church and Christendom into a new period. Into a better future?

The theory of the faith: Professor Dr. Joseph Ratzinger in the late 1950s, lecturing at the Philosophical and Theological Academy in Freising near Munich. He saw the end of the war as a decisive moment for Christianity.

A journey into the past: in 1997, Joseph Ratzinger visits the house of his parents in Marktl am Inn. He stands beside his cradle in the room where he was born on April 16, 1927.

My Brother the Pope

Habemus papam, habemus papam! On April 19, 2005, as the loudest shouts of joy in all its history shook the venerable cathedral of Regensburg, one man sat alone before the television set, only a few minutes' walking distance away. He was in a turmoil of emotions. He was Georg Ratzinger (eighty-one), former music director for the cathedral, the older brother of the man who had just been elected Pope.

At this moment, he was the loneliest man in the world. While 1.1 billion Catholics—one-sixth of the world's population—were rejoicing that they had received their new head, Georg Ratzinger sat in his armchair in a state of "shock": "I have lost the companion for the evening of my life!"

They had planned to spend their years of retirement together in their Bavarian homeland. Instead, he would now visit Benedict XVI (seventy-eight) in Rome "from time to time": "Perhaps twice a year", he says in a conversation in his simple apartment in the ancient city center of Regensburg.

Did he weep when he heard the conclave's decision?

"No, I never weep", the former conductor of the Regensburg Domspatzen choir replies in his Bavarian dialect. But he was "very sad" when his brother suddenly waved at him from the television as the newly elected Pope. "I have never seen him so depressed", whispers his faithful housekeeper, Agnes Heindl

"I have lost the companion for the evening of my life!"

(eighty). He told her to disconnect the telephone—and this meant that when Pope Benedict XVI tried to ring his "big brother" on the evening of his election, he could not get through. It was only next morning that he was able to speak to Georg, who was in a very real sense "harder to get hold of than the Pope".

Their roots are inseparably intertwined. They grew up together, both became altar boys ("I cannot recall Joseph ever having missed a Mass"), and both submitted with great reluctance to the coercions of the Nazi dictatorship: Joseph as a member of the Hitler Youth and anti-aircraft auxiliary, Georg as a radio operator in Italy.

After the war, when they were both free, they embraced each other. "In those months, we often played piano duets. That was a wonderful time."

Both men decided to serve God and the Church, and they received priestly ordination together in the summer of 1951. What happened after their ways parted? "We exchanged letters regularly. Later, we telephoned at least once a week." There is only one thing they have never done in all these years: "We have never heard each other's confessions." In very simple, warm-hearted words, Georg Ratzinger talks of the holiday they spent together in Regensburg in 2004: "It was always wonderful when he was there—especially on Sunday, when he came straight after the early Mass. The first thing he did was to swallow his 'poison'. That is

On holiday with his brother. Each year, Georg Ratzinger (*left*) visits his famous brother in Rome. In 1995, they made an excursion to the ruins of the temple of Paestum in southern Italy.

what he always says when he has to take his medicines with a glass of water."

Thanks to an eye complaint, Georg Ratzinger is "almost blind". He is all the more grateful to his brother for reading important theological texts aloud to him. "He has often read the prayers aloud for me. Then we would listen to music—a symphony on the radio, or CDs of Mozart, Haydn, Bach, or Beethoven. Or a recording by the Domspatzen. My brother, too, appreciates them."

For lunch, the Cardinal from Rome usually asked for some kind of pastry dish in the Bavarian or Salzburg tradition, which Mrs. Heindl prepared. After this, the brothers would rest, then visit the grave of their parents.

In the evening, they would walk out to the simple detached house of the Cardinal at Pentling, a suburb of Regensburg. There they would have a cold supper: "bread with sausage or cheese". But what were they to do with the dishes?

"His tidy desk shows that my brother is a man who keeps good order and does not have things lying around", says Georg Ratzinger. They solved the problem together: "I dried." The Cardinal washed.

Georg Ratzinger smiles almost imperceptibly as he shares his memories with you. But he takes a very different tone if you mention the attacks to which his brother has sometimes been exposed. Then his gray eyebrows come together like storm clouds: "Nonsense!" he growls about the headlines in the British press that accused the Pope of having a past in the Hitler Youth. And he recom-

"Sometimes he loses things. All of a sudden, he doesn't know where his watch is, or his key, or some particular document"

mends to his fellow Germans that they should not always ask what his brother is "against" (women priests, feminism, a relaxation of the celibacy law). Instead, they should also ask what he is "for": "For a life lived in faith and for a deep union with the Eucharist."

The older brother protects the younger: sometimes, he thinks that critics of Joseph's faithfulness to his own principles are "like little children who are not content with anything but always want something new. Why not simply accept the limitations that our faith imposes on us, when these are in keeping with the nature of things and are the clear will of God?"

He knows him better than anyone else, so he must know: Does the new Pope have any weaknesses? After a long pause for thought, only one point occurs to Georg Ratzinger: "Sometimes he loses things. All of a sudden he doesn't know where his watch is, or his key, or some particular document."

He admires most of all the "intellectual clarity" of his brother, his patience, and the fact "that we help each other". For almost eight decades, they have gone together through thick and thin.

They have never actually spoken of "brotherly love", but "that is absolutely the right word." Even when they disagree, Georg cannot think ill of Joseph—not even now that the plan to spend the evening of their lives together will not be realized: "That would be egoism on my part. And besides, I am convinced that the call to become Pope is not merely a human decision. It was the will of God."

"Not as if we ourselves could do anything on our own: our capability comes from God" (2 Cor 3:5).

"From his fullness we have all received, grace upon grace" (Jn 1:16).

...ough the grace of God at the altar of ordination and the first solemn Mass.

Freising June 29	**1951**	Traunstein July 8
Joseph Ratzinger		**Georg Ratzinger**

My brother the Pope: Georg Ratzinger (81), retired music director of the Regensburg cathedral, proudly displays the headline in the *Bild*. The brothers were ordained to the priesthood in 1951, but they celebrated their first solemn Masses separately (*see photograph left*).

Pope Benedict XVI greets his brother Georg as he passes by in the "popemobile" in Saint Peter's Square.

The brothers Joseph and
Georg Ratzinger meet
again in their Bavarian
homeland, this time in
Traunstein, where both
once attended junior
seminary. Coffee and
cakes were served to the
distinguished visitor from
Rome—Benedict XVI is
fond of sweet pastries.

A Life for God

The war was over; the clock read 00:00. Some people felt mostly shame; some were simply concerned with surviving. Others again—the persecuted, the democrats, the Christians who had refused to compromise—were looking for the right way to start anew.

In 1946, around 120 seminarians, famished in both the material and the intellectual sense, lived in the seminary in Freising. Their ages ranged from nineteen to forty. The rector had spent five years in the concentration camp at Dachau.

One important influence on Ratzinger's position was his roots in the faith of his parents, in a rural, liberal-Bavarian piety. Another influence was the experience of the Nazi terror, of war and genocide. These two came together in the young student. Ratzinger writes, "In the faith of my parents I found the confirmation that Catholicism had been a bulwark of truth and justice against that regime of atheism and falsehood." There was a sense of a new departure, and the young man was eager "to make up for lost time and to serve Christ in his Church for a new and better age; for a better Germany, for a better world."

The regional author Georg Lohmeier, a fellow student, relates: "Even as early as the years in Freising, Joe was noticeable for his acute intellect and his gift of formulation. He was very serious and didn't say much. I

"Even then, I thought: Joe will be a doctor of the Church one day" (Georg Lohmeier, a fellow student)

thought even then that he might perhaps become a doctor of the Church."

Ratzinger did not want to study theology as one might study the tools of any profession. His aim was "to understand the faith".

His studies concentrated initially on Heidegger, who gave the young Ratzinger the feeling "that one can glimpse the clearing in the woods, despite the various wrong paths", Jaspers, the Jewish thinker Martin Buber, and especially one of the really great men of the Church: Augustine, a man of artistic sensibilities, a strict and systematic theologian, whose stormy life finally reached the harbor of wisdom and adoration. He is "in a very direct way the passionate, suffering, questioning human being, with whom one can identify".

On September 1, 1947, after completing the study of philosophy, Ratzinger began his theological studies in the seminary of the University of Munich, which had been evacuated to Fürstenried. Lectures were held in a garden greenhouse, but the lack of equipment was more than compensated for by the quality of the teachers, who were the best at that time. Ratzinger was fascinated: "I found it wonderful to penetrate the great world of the history of the faith. Broad horizons of thinking and believing opened up before me, and I learned how to reflect both on the fundamental questions of human existence and on my own existential questions."

The young priest, who will become Pope fifty-three years later. In 1952, Joseph Ratzinger celebrates Mass with hikers on a mountain near Ruhpolding.

FROM JOSEPH RATZINGER TO POPE BENEDICT XVI

Ratzinger explains one of the constant concerns of his life as follows: the attempt to enter into the thought of the great masters of the faith, but "not to stop short in the ancient Church. I wanted to get below the encrustations, to expose the real kernel of the faith, and thus give it fresh power and dynamism." Although the basic direction of his life was clear, doubts still remained. After all, "men and women students lived at close quarters" in Fürstenried Castle, so that "the question of renunciation and of its inner meaning had a very practical character." In this "period of great decisions, which were made at the cost of suffering", it became clear to him "that the call to the priesthood involves more than the delight in theology". Could he observe celibacy all his life long? Could he deal with people; could he be a pastor for the elderly and the sick? Could he inspire young Catholics?

Another problem he faced was the question of truth. "In view of all our limitations", is it not presumptuous to claim "that we could know truth"? At some point, however, the decision was made. There was indeed "no lightning flash of illumination all in a single moment", since the decision "grew slowly as I myself grew and had to be pondered and made again and again." Nevertheless, he describes his definitive call to the priesthood as the irruption of a power outside himself: "I was convinced—though I myself do not know how—that God wanted something from me that could be achieved only if I became a priest."

The great day of his priestly ordination came on June 29, 1951, in the cathedral of Freising. At the summons of Cardinal Faulhaber, the candidate replied: "*Adsum*—Here I am." It was a radiant summer day that Ratzinger experienced as "the high point of my whole life". One event in particular became engraved on his memory. He relates that, while one ought not to be superstitious, "Just

"I was convinced that God wanted something from me that could be achieved only if I became a priest"

at the moment when the aged archbishop laid his hands on me, a little bird—perhaps a lark—soared up from the high altar into the lofty cathedral and trilled a little song of exultation. It was as if a voice from heaven assured me: 'All is well, you are on the right path.'"

Ratzinger's teacher and supporter was the theologian Gottfried Söhngen, a cheerful Rhinelander who was the child of a "mixed marriage" and was actively involved in the ecumenical question. Söhngen rightly divined the inclinations and gifts of his protégé and provided decisive impulses by suggesting the themes for his doctoral dissertation and his professorial dissertation [*Habilitation*]: "People and House of God in Augustine's Doctrine of the Church" and "The Historical Theology of Saint Bonaventure".

Another professor, the famous Michael Schmaus, suspected that Ratzinger was a dangerous modernizer. Not only that: Schmaus was a highly respected scholar, and Ratzinger had dared to criticize him.

As joint examiner, Schmaus rejected the professorial dissertation, and this was a tremendous blow to Ratzinger: "I felt that the whole world was collapsing around me." What would now become of his parents "if I had to leave the university as a failure"? Schmaus told him smugly that he would doubtless need a year to revise his work, but Ratzinger submitted it again within a fortnight—and this time successfully.

Immediately after taking his doctorate, he began work in a parish. From August 1951, he was curate in the parish of the Precious Blood in Munich and preached up to three sermons each Sunday, heard confessions every morning, celebrated weddings and baptisms, went on his bicycle to funerals, and gave religious instruction in school. His parish priest, Msgr. Blumschein, told him that a priest must "glow", and Ratzinger enjoyed "emerging from the intellectual world and learning how to talk to children".

Ora et labora, pray and work. In 1960, the young Professor Joseph Ratzinger prepares a lecture in the library of the seminary in Bonn. He teaches dogmatics at the University of Bonn.

A brilliant mind, a spartan life:
Professor Joseph Ratzinger
in 1959 in his sparely
furnished room with a piano
and a portable typewriter.

61

FROM JOSEPH RATZINGER TO POPE BENEDICT XVI

As professor of dogmatic theology, Ratzinger taught first in Bonn and later in Münster, Tübingen, and Regensburg. Bonn was the place he had "dreamed of". The young professor enjoyed "the thriving academic life" at the faculty in Bonn. At night, he heard the ships passing by on the Rhine, the river that gave him "a feeling of openness and breadth". The students admired their professor for his attempts "to relate clearly as much as possible of the curriculum to the present day and to our own struggles".

This period was saddened by the sudden death of his father. Ratzinger was profoundly affected, sensing "that the world had become emptier for me and that a part of my 'home' had been translated to the world to come." When his mother, too, died in the following years, Ratzinger experienced once more the phenomenon that he believed he had observed on the death of his father: "Her goodness had become even purer and more radiant." He drew the conclusion that "there is no more convincing proof of the faith" than the pure humanity we see in those who have come to full maturity in the faith.

The Second Vatican Council brought a new sphere of activity for Ratzinger. He was

His parish priest told him: "A priest must glow", and Ratzinger liked this sentiment

appointed adviser to Cardinal Frings of Cologne and later became an official conciliar theologian and, thereby, one of those who completely overturned the original plans for the Council. Increasingly, however, the young scholar had the impression "that nothing in the Church was really stable—everything was up for grabs." Ratzinger's position changed. One had expected "a leap forward", but all that came was "a process of decline".

The student movement of the 1960s did not bypass theologians. To begin with, Ratzinger could sympathize with "the protest against a pragmatism born of material prosperity", but ultimately, he could not close his eyes to "every kind of terror, from a subtle psychological terrorization to open violence". Even theologians mocked the crucified Savior in caricatures as a sadomasochist. In these years, he learned "when a discussion must stop, because it is turning into a lie; and when one must offer resistance, in order to maintain freedom".

In 1969, he accepted a professorship at Regensburg, which he had earlier turned down. He now believed that he had found his "own theological vision" and that he could begin creating a theological work of his own: "I knew that I was called to a life of scholarship."

June 29, 1951: ordination to the priesthood in Freising cathedral near Munich. In his memoirs, Joseph Ratzinger (who was ordained that day together with his brother) calls it: "A summer day that remains unforgettable as the high point of my whole life."

He Showed Us the Way to God's Love

By ELMAR GRUBER

When he gave his first lecture in the Academy of Freising in 1954, Ratzinger entered the classroom, which was full of students. He was pale but assured. I can still remember the subject of his lecture: truth is a person. Truth is known through love. "For me, theology is the attempt to get to know the Beloved better." For myself, as for many of my fellow students, these words became a leitmotif for our studies and for our work as priests.

Ratzinger usually spoke without any written notes. He never stumbled, never corrected himself, never repeated himself. If one took notes—though one was initially reluctant to do so—one discovered a crystal-clear theoretical construction. During vacations, I learned many of his sentences by heart, in order to acquire at least something of his brilliant use of words.

The special novelty in his discourse was (and is) the fascinating use of images, signs, and symbols, which allowed him to lead us far more deeply into the mystery of God than if he had employed rational definitions. His great strength is meditative, reflective thinking (emotional intelligence). This kindled tremendous enthusiasm in those who heard him. His rational brilliance, linked with his verbal gifts, generated an unconditional admiration.

Elmar Gruber (74) studied theology under Joseph Ratzinger in Freising and was ordained priest in 1957.

Ratzinger as Preacher

It was customary at that time for one of the Academy professors to preach on the Sundays in May. The cathedral was packed when Ratzinger ascended the pulpit, and all listened to his words in a breathless silence.

I noticed some professors creeping into the cathedral by a side door, as if they were embarrassed at the thought of being recognized while listening to their young colleague—at that time, he was still under thirty.

Whether it was a sermon, a meditation, or a lecture, one was always moved, fascinated, and consoled. And one looked forward to the next meeting with him.

Ratzinger as Examiner

A fellow student and I once had our examination in vacation time in the apartment of the Ratzinger family. His father opened the door, and my colleague blurted out: "Mr. Ratzinger, I hope you will put in a good word for us with your son. We are just about to have our examination!" Mr. Ratzinger replied, "No, I never do that. I just say, 'Joey, be fair!'"

Ratzinger's knowledge was simply boundless. But he was also aware of what his students knew and what they did not know. He always asked the candidates about topics they knew. This is how I got top marks in

Three friends who became priests. Joseph Ratzinger (*right*), his brother, Georg (*left*), and their friend Rupert Berger after the ordination on June 29, 1951.

A striking face, a
brilliant intellect.
Joseph Ratzinger
as professor and
theologian of the
Second Vatican
Council.

dogmatics! And ultimately, it is thanks to him that I was able to complete my studies. I have a bad memory for dates, and the professors in the Academy wanted to fail me. Ratzinger pleaded on my behalf, and I was allowed to stay on in the seminary and to become a priest.

Ratzinger as Professor

Once, on the feast of Saint Corbinian, the founder of the church in Freising, a great number of parish priests, monsignors, deans (with red skull-caps), and chamberlains (with blue skull-caps) had assembled for the procession into the cathedral. The young Professor Ratzinger stood to one side, and those who did not know him might easily have assumed him to be a seminarian. Suddenly, an elderly and overweight dean— doubtless beloved by God—began to grumble and bawled out the startled professor because he had not greeted the dean with sufficient obsequiousness. Ratzinger offered his apologies. The dean continued his grumbling and said to us seminarians: "What kind of an idiot do you have there, eh?" When we replied, "Well, Your Reverence, that is our dogmatics professor", the dean must have wished the earth could open up and swallow him . . .

Ratzinger as Chief Fireman

In the seminary, one apartment was reserved for a teacher who gave some courses in our house and was also responsible for our domestic fire brigade. Ratzinger held this post for a time. One hot summer afternoon, while we were supposed to be studying, we had the idea of holding a fire brigade exercise instead. We thought out our arguments and attempted to convince our chief fireman that this exercise was necessary. It was not easy, but at last Ratzinger gave us his blessing. This,

however, did not turn the water in our hoses into "holy water": we rolled out the hoses and in no time at all, the inner courtyard was under water. Someone was heard to use the biblical expression: "Flood!"

"Just Like in a Hotel"—An Evening Meal with Ratzinger

My brother was secretary to Cardinal Döpfner (died 1976) during the Council and afterward became his vicar general. At that time, my brother and I lived in our parents' house in the Laim suburb of Munich, and I looked after domestic affairs. When Ratzinger succeeded Döpfner, we invited him to supper, and he did in fact come. I was very proud of this: "What will people say when they see the bishop getting out of his car in front of our house!"

"For me, theology is the attempt to get to know the Beloved better"

I made the meal. The menu was steaks, rice, salad, and fruit salad. Ratzinger commented: "Just like in a hotel!" I am still proud of those words. After we had eaten, I admired his patience even more, when he had to look at my brother's slides from Bolivia!

I met Ratzinger once again on the fortieth anniversary of my priestly ordination, when he celebrated a thanksgiving Mass for us and with us. The past does not pass away, even when our paths diverge.

Shepherd and Fisherman

The good shepherd remains with the sheep when he sees the wolf coming. His love is for all the sheep, even the sheep in another fold, even the black sheep! The fisherman who fishes only for his own interest catches nothing. But one who sets out the nets "at your word" need not trouble to fish, since the fish will come by themselves, all 153 of them, all of them, all of them, and the net will not break.

Dear Holy Father, we give thanks that God has called you to this ministry.

Co-Workers of the Truth

By PETER SEEWALD

"Work in God's field!" With these words, Pope Paul VI asked the professor to go to Munich. In March 1977, Joseph Ratzinger was ordained Archbishop of Munich, as successor to the deceased Julius Döpfner.

It was the day before Pentecost, a glorious day in early summer. The cathedral was beautifully decorated with flowers, and the faithful gave him a tremendous welcome on the Marienplatz. Ratzinger recalls that "the whole atmosphere was somehow irresistible. I experienced what a sacrament is—that in the sacraments, reality takes place."

The words in which he evokes the historical character of that day show the depth of his feelings: "With episcopal ordination, the present day begins in my biography. That which began with the laying on of hands for episcopal ordination in the cathedral of Munich is still the present-day reality of my life."

This was a time of great upheavals in society, and old traditions were considered dusty and obsolete. A new prosperity led the middle classes to close their eyes to the wider world, while young people rebelled against bourgeois smugness and capitalism. In Germany, the Red Army Faction (RTF [a left-wing insurgent organization]) began its bloody fight against democracy.

The Church, too, was affected by social changes—resulting in a slackening in the faith, a reduced number of vocations, and a lowering of moral standards even among the faithful. Precisely at the beginning of his episcopal ministry, says Joseph Ratzinger, "the words of the Bible and the Church Fathers echoed continuously in my ears. They vigorously condemn shepherds who are like dumb dogs and are so concerned to avoid conflicts that they allow the poison to spread." The truth is "that the Church must never enter an alliance with the zeitgeist. She must address the vices and perils of each historical period." He finds a bishop "whose only aim is to avoid trouble a terrifying vision."

His episcopal motto, borrowed from Augustine [and 3 John 8], is: "Co-Workers of the Truth". There can be no more demanding program than that. He declared this principle as soon as he became bishop: "Calm is not the primary duty of a citizen", and he became a "cornerstone" from this point in his life onward, just like Jesus himself, the "cornerstone" whom the builders could not fit into their preconceived ideas and therefore rejected. Ten years before this, Ratzinger had criticized the decrepit structures of the Church. Now, he continually warned against the newly awakened centrifugal forces, since he was afraid they might tear society apart.

Ratzinger attacked the "pollution of the intellectual environment, which we can see in the growing number of children with behavioral disorders", the "fatty degeneration of the heart thanks to wealth and hedonism", and the "capitalist lust for profit". At Easter, he raised his voice against "the unleashing of violence and the reduction of

A theologian and teacher of the faith becomes a bishop. Joseph Stangl places the miter on the head of Joseph Ratzinger at his ordination as Bishop of Munich in 1977.

In humility he prostrates himself before the challenge of his new ministry. Joseph Ratzinger seeks strength in prayer. During his episcopal ordination, after promising fidelity, he lies on the altar steps while the litany is sung.

human beings to the state of barbarians, which we see everywhere in the world". And as far as the Church is concerned, "one of the most urgent tasks for Christians is to recover the ability to be nonconformist, that is, the ability to oppose a whole number of developments in our contemporary culture."

People listened to Ratzinger. The media might dismiss his warnings as too apocalyptic, but ordinary people felt he was truly talking to them. Fifty thousand copies of his Lenten pastoral letter were ordered from the diocesan curia after it was published in May 1980.

Three months after he was ordained to the episcopate, Joseph Ratzinger was created a cardinal by Paul VI. He was one of the youngest members of this worldwide college. It was at this time that he met a man who was to leave his mark on Ratzinger's biography. In a meeting with Karol Cardinal Wojtyla, Archbishop of Krakow, he resolved that Germans and Poles ought to take "the path toward each other" in a more resolute manner. These two bishops inspired each other and became allies. "I have always quite spontaneously had a good relationship with him", said Ratzinger. He was impressed by Wojtyla's "uncomplicated human directness and openness and by the warmth he radiates. He is humorous, he is pious—and one senses that nothing is artificial." Karol Wojtyla went to Rome as Pope John Paul II, and Joseph Ratzinger remained in Munich—for the time being.

Even while a diocesan bishop, Ratzinger led the Catholic Church through stormy times. He celebrates Mass at the German national Catholic Assembly in Freiburg in 1978.

As bishop, he upheld the position of his Church against abortion and defended the Pope against criticism. The Church cannot simply accept today's opinions; rather, "in view of the evil in the world, she must proclaim the medicine of the Gospel."

Nevertheless, the *Süddeutsche Zeitung* (Munich's leading newspaper) praised him in these terms: "Of all the conservatives in the Church, he is the one with the strongest capacity for dialogue." Some admired him as a guardian of the right values, while his critics saw him as the personification of a rigid Church.

Ratzinger is a Bavarian patriot. His handkerchief has a pattern of blue and white. "Our

Bavaria is so beautiful", he has said, "because the Christian faith awakened its best abilities." Thanks to the Christian heritage, "our people have an attitude toward life in which we see that true 'liberality' where tolerance has become recognition and recognition has become tolerance."

His time in his beloved homeland was soon to end. In 1981, John Paul II appointed him Prefect of the Congregation for the Doctrine of the Faith—one of the most important, but also one of the most unpopular, offices in the Catholic Church.

Ratzinger was aware of the heavy burden entailed by the office of guardian of the faith.

At supper, he told his brother of the Pope's decision: "I heard today that I have to go to Rome. For good."

The container took to Rome a walnut writing desk he had inherited from his parents, a piano, and two thousand books.

He knew that difficult times awaited him. In a sermon delivered before his departure from Munich, he said that it had become dark around him. He wanted to be like everyone else, just to be himself—but he knew that not all the future news would be cheerful.

He asked his fellow Bavarians: "Let us keep together! Let us remain united!"

The faithful greet him joyfully: Archbishop Ratzinger is acclaimed by enthusiastic Catholics in Munich in 1977.

In the quieter moments of his taxing episcopal ministry, Joseph Ratzinger sits down at his piano and plays Mozart and Bach—here, for friends in Annecy.

He Plays Mozart and Reads Steppenwolf

When the Pope wants to relax, he sits down at his piano and plays Mozart. Since his childhood, he has been a fan of the musical genius (1756–1791). "Mozart touches something very deep in me, because his music is so brilliant and at the same time so profound. It is not just a game: it contains the entire tragic dimension of the human person." Besides Mozart, the new Pope loves the music of

Johann Sebastian Bach (1685–1750) and Giovanni Pierluigi da Palestrina (1525–1594). As a young man, he wrote poems about "things in everyday life, poems about Christmas and nature". Ratzinger says: "This indicates the pleasure I took in expressing myself." His favorite book is Hermann Hesse's *Steppenwolf*. Benedict XVI also loves animals, especially cats. He has spoken out against cruel and unnecessary experiments on animals: "They, too, are God's creatures. Animals are entrusted to our protection. We cannot simply do anything we like with them."

The faithful love him, and celebrities are attracted by his brilliant intellect. Joseph Ratzinger with the actress Ruth Leuwerik.

Talking to Jesus ... Cardinal Ratzinger with the actors who played Mary and Jesus at the Oberammergau Passion Play in 1980.

Congratulations from Bavaria: on Ratzinger's seventy-fifth birthday, 350 Mountain Guards came to Rome. Here, their commander congratulates the Cardinal.

"I Am a Bavarian"

"My roots remain; I am a Bavarian", said the Holy Father at his first audience. Born and baptized in Marktl am Inn (2,700 inhabitants), Joseph Ratzinger has visited his homeland regularly for many years. He reads the *Mittelbayrische Zeitung* from Regensburg every day in Rome. His birthplace, the boarding school he attended in Traunstein (with its five churches and nine chapels), and Altötting: here, in "God's corner" of Bavaria, lie the roots of the piety of Benedict XVI. With his father, the young Ratzinger often went on foot to the famous Marian pilgrimage shrine. He once said: "Altötting is the heart of Bavaria and one of the hearts of Europe." It was here that his decision to become a priest took form. He is deeply rooted in the everyday piety of Bavarian Catholicism. His path has taken him from the Chiemgau region to the Vatican: "The Catholicism of my native land has understood how to accommodate everything that is human: prayer as well as feasting, penitence as well as cheerfulness."

A bishop who defends the faith—and a real Bavarian. After formally blessing a new convent building, Joseph Ratzinger enjoys a sip from a beer stein.

A churchman whom the people love. The faithful cheer Joseph Ratzinger outside his residence after his ordination as Archbishop of Munich (1977).

A brother and intimate friend. In his more than thirty years as director of cathedral music, Georg Ratzinger gave over 1,000 concerts with the Regensburg Domspatzen. His brother Joseph was often in the audience.

Support in faith, support in the family. Joseph Cardinal Ratzinger with his sister, Maria (who died in 1991), at a concert of the Regensburg Domspatzen.

Farewell, Munich! Ratzinger bids the faithful farewell on the Marienplatz in Munich, when he goes to Rome in 1982 (*above*).

At the early age of fifty, he is created cardinal by Pope Paul VI (*right*).

When he leaves Munich, the Bavarian Prime Minister Franz Josef Strauss gives him a crucifix as a parting gift (*far right*).

The Bavarian Mountain Guards have arrived, and Joseph Cardinal Ratzinger tests the sharpness of the commander's saber. It is a time of farewell, only a few days before the Cardinal leaves for Rome.

83

Il tedesco—A German in Rome

By PETER SEEWALD

Joseph Cardinal Ratzinger arrived in the Eternal City in the spring of 1982. In addition to his German citizenship, he now received a passport of the Vatican City, the world's smallest state.

As Prefect of the Congregation for the Doctrine of the Faith, he earned a monthly salary of about 2,600 dollars. He lived in a small apartment (less than 1000 square feet) very close to the apostolic palace, and he could be seen at nine o'clock each morning, wearing his soutane, as he walked across Saint Peter's Square with his shabby black briefcase. He had two offices for his work.

The Romans called the new man "Il tedesco—the German". Ratzinger had not only the burden of his office but also the burden of recent German history to bear. He says: "There are well-known ideas about Germans. That is why some people are tempted to ascribe unpopular decisions to German pig-headedness. A fanatical attachment to principles, a lack of flexibility—all that is seen as typically German. The person who invented the expression 'panzer cardinal' was doubtless also making that kind of allusion to German national characteristics."

He began to like Rome. When not working, he took little walks in the Borgo Pio, chatting to the fruit sellers and talking to the cats. In his free time, he played the piano or worked on lectures and sermons, especially for his friends in Germany—and if a bishop was needed, he held confirmations in their parishes, too.

He and Pope John Paul II were a harmonious team. One was emotional, vigorous, with the talents of a media star; the other was the brilliant thinker, utterly solid and reliable, even if there were different interpretations in the assessment of some questions. The Spanish author Juan Arias has written that neither of them "can really be called a man who does not live in our world. Neither of them is a theological reactionary. On the contrary, they are intelligent reformers who are completely correct to feel that they are progressives who support Vatican II."

Ratzinger accepted his new task, which he defined at the beginning of his period in office as "thinking and offering help in this difficult situation for the Church and doing whatever I can". A primary task was "the dialogue with theology and with theologians".

Things turned out differently, however. The case of Hans Küng, who had been his colleague as a professor in Tübingen, was fortunately already settled, but the proceedings against Leonardo Boff, the Brazilian liberation theologian, proved exceedingly difficult.

Boff had proclaimed that "the thinking of the historical Jesus does not envisage the Church as an institution." Ratzinger admonished him to reflect on this subject for a year

"I was already a cardinal when I came to Rome. This meant that I did not need to play for power or to wonder about my future career prospects"

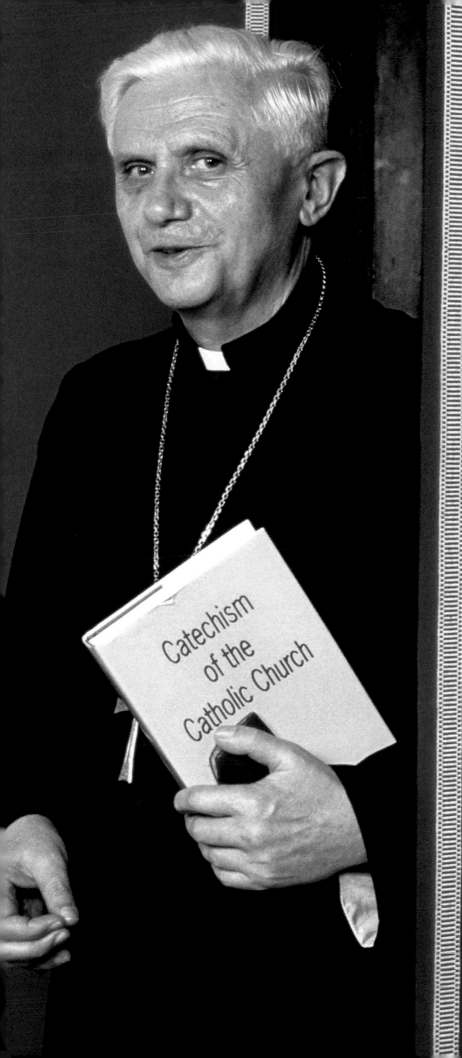

A book that cost him five years of his life. In his hand, Joseph Cardinal Ratzinger holds the *Catechism of the Catholic Church*, which he drew up as Prefect of the Congregation for the Doctrine of the Faith. In the United States alone, two million copies of the English edition have been sold.

During his years as Prefect of the Congregation for the Doctrine of the Faith, Joseph Cardinal Ratzinger often returned to his homeland. In 1990, he celebrates Mass to mark the two thousandth anniversary of the city of Speyer.

The Congregation for the Doctrine of the Faith

The Congregation is responsible for questions of ethics and of the faith. It was founded by Pope Paul III on July 21, 1542, as the "Congregation of the Roman and General Inquisition". Its task was to protect the Church from errors, in order that the message of the Gospel might be handed on free of all falsification. In 1908, its name was changed to "Sacred Congregation of the Holy Office". In 1988, Pope John Paul II defined its duties as follows: "to promote and protect the doctrine of faith and morals throughout the Catholic Church". It was to devote more attention to the promotion of the doctrines of the faith than to tasks of inspection and supervision. The Congregation has twenty-five members. Naturally, since it is the decisive body under the Pope in all questions of Church doctrine, it often attracts media attention. Cardinal Ratzinger headed the Congregation from 1981 until the death of John Paul II. He was often criticized and labeled a "Grand Inquisitor" because of his interpretation of the faith.

After praying in church,
Ratzinger, head of the Congregation for the Doctrine of
the Faith, heads back to his
forty colleagues.

On the rooftops
of the Eternal
City. In 1993,
shortly after
suffering a super-
ficial wound in a
fall, Ratzinger
stands on a roof
terrace near Saint
Peter's basilica.

They were companions and became friends. In November 1980, Cardinal Ratzinger welcomed Pope John Paul II to Munich.

A Star Named Ratzinger

As cardinal, Ratzinger opened up to scholars the archives of the Inquisition. For the first time in the history of the Church, researchers could study original documents in her possession.

This led astronomers to honor him by giving asteroid no. 8661 the name "Ratzinger". This asteroid is about ten kilometers in size and is one of the many mini-planets that circle the sun between Mars and Jupiter. Its position lies

exactly between the asteroids Sano and Daun-Eifel. Its distance from the earth is 3.751 AU (1 Astronomical Unit = about 93 million miles), that is, 1,460 times the distance between the earth and the moon.

GUARDIAN OF THE FAITH

and not to speak publicly about it during this period. This measure provoked worldwide criticism, and the Prefect of the Congregation for the Doctrine of the Faith had now definitively acquired the reputation of a hardliner.

Controversial positions had long taken shape within the Catholic Church. In particular, German professors of theology who saw themselves as especially progressive opposed what they called "reactionary Roman centralism". From now on, every one of the disputed topics—celibacy, abortion, the dogma of infallibility, homosexuality, contraception—provided ammunition for a personal attack on the guardian of the faith.

"I was already a cardinal when I came to Rome. This meant that I did not need to play for power or to wonder about my future career prospects." He explained patiently that he would "never dare to impose my own theological ideas on Christendom by means of the decisions taken by the Congregation". Such decisions were always arrived at in a worldwide collaboration with bishops, theologians, and special commissions.

Ratzinger saw his own role as akin to that of the ancient Church Fathers such as Saint Athanasius, who fought against the errors of his time in order to keep safe for future generations the message of the Gospel. The official definition of his task was "to promote sound doctrine, correct errors, and bring the erring back to the right path". This task made enormous demands of the Prefect. A friend said: "He uses enormous resources of strength to go against the tide. He takes his task seriously—too seriously." Eugen Biser, a liberal theologian in Munich, was one of the few who assessed Ratzinger's situation with Christian compassion as early as 1993: "When the final reckoning is made, we will see that he prevented many things and toned down others. And we will see that he has sacrificed to his ecclesiastical office more of his own feelings and his own happiness than we can imagine."

At his audience each Friday, the Cardinal discussed current ecclesiastical business with

He guarded the faith in stormy times. Joseph Cardinal Ratzinger in October 1981, on the snowy Zugspitze Mountain.

Ratzinger's life is dedicated to the serious business of the faith, but he, too, enjoys a joke. In 1989, the Order of Karl Valentin is bestowed on him during the Carnival.

the Pope. Especially difficult cases were discussed over supper; they spoke German with each other.

In 1986, the Holy Father commissioned him to produce a new catechism—a mammoth task that was to entail five years' hard work. "Naturally, it is a human book, which could certainly be improved", he was to say later. "But it is a good book!" And John Paul II was to praise its publication as "one of the most important events of recent Church history".

In 1991, shortly before the book was completed, Cardinal Ratzinger suffered a mild

stroke. He spent a month in the hospital and must still take low-dose anticoagulant aspirin. He paid the price for his work. At the time, Joseph Cardinal Ratzinger said: "This life is very hard. I am waiting impatiently for the time when I can write a few more books."

As we know, the Pope refused to let him retire. He wanted to cross the threshold of the new millennium for the Church together with Joseph Ratzinger, and the Cardinal accepted this.

He was to remain at the Pope's side until the latter's death.

The princess and
the cardinal. Gloria
of Thurn and Taxis
with her son Albert
meets Joseph Rat-
zinger in 1984.

The guardian of the faith in the sacred halls of the Vatican. Ratzinger had his office here as Prefect of the Congregation for the Doctrine of the Faith. He often worked for hours on end, without a break and without eating anything.

The Handmaid of God

By PETER SEEWALD

On a day of mourning, Ingrid Stampa came to work for Cardinal Joseph Ratzinger. And she stayed there.

In 1991, his sister, Maria, who had been his housekeeper for thirty years, died. Her death left Joseph Ratzinger, Prefect of the Congregation for the Doctrine of the Faith, alone in his 1000 square-foot apartment above the rooftops of Rome. There was no one to look after it for him.

The personal physician of Pope John Paul II, Renato Buzzonetti, asked an acquaintance to take this position: Ingrid Stampa, formerly professor of music at the Academy of Music in Hamburg, a cultured woman who is a virtuoso on the *viola da gamba* (a predecessor of the cello) and has given many concerts. She speaks Polish fluently and has translated the books of Pope John Paul II into German. Since the end of the 1980s, she had lived in Rome. Many years earlier, she had given away all her possessions, including her musical instruments, in order to care for a friend in the Eternal City who had cancer. That was the end of one phase in her life.

She had a profound love of music. Her profession was difficult but also very beautiful, and she was devoted to it. For the sake of her music, she led a life as strict as a nun's and sacrificed everything else to this. One could say that she was married to music.

Since 1991, she has dedicated her "monastic" life-style completely to looking after the Cardinal. To begin with, she cooked Italian meals for him, but then she learned to make the favorite dishes of his Bavarian homeland: apple strudel, sweet dumplings, and bread dumplings. She created for him a place for silent meditation in the loggia of his apartment, a garden she tended with care. She went shopping on her bicycle.

Soon, the guardian of the faith and the music professor enjoyed a good friendship marked by trust and respect.

At some point, the Lord broke into her life and demanded that she decide whether she wanted to pursue her career—and hence live for her own self—or whether she was willing to let herself fall totally into God's hands, so that she would henceforth serve God alone, wherever he might want her to be.

At some point, the Lord broke into her life

Her decision was clear: she remained at the side of the man who interprets the will of God.

When Ratzinger worked indefatigably on the documents of the Congregation for the Doctrine of the Faith, she brought sandwiches to his desk, but he usually left these untouched until his work was finished. When the Cardinal needed something, he rang the secret number of her cell phone. She continued to work on translations for John Paul II. Just as she was finishing the German version of his book *Memory and Identity*, life took a new turn. The Pope did not recover from his grave illness: John Paul II died, and the conclave elected her "boss" as the new Pope. April 19, 2005, changed her whole life.

GUARDIAN OF THE FAITH

Ingrid Stampa (55) has been Joseph Ratzinger's housekeeper since 1991. She was professor at the Academy of Music in Hamburg and gave up her career in the world in order to serve God alone.

The woman behind the Pope: Benedict XVI visits the papal apartment in the Vatican (*photograph above*). In a black dress with white collar, we see Ingrid Stampa, the Holy Father's housekeeper. *Left:* Ingrid Stampa with the Pope's brother, Georg Ratzinger, who was visiting the Vatican. *Far left:* The housekeeper passes one of the Swiss Guard on her way to work.

GUARDIAN OF THE FAITH

We can picture the day: she was working at her computer when she saw the white smoke. She ran to Saint Peter's Square and tried to ring a friend to find out who had been elected—but the cell phone network had broken down. When she stood on the Square and heard the words *Josephum cardinalem Ratzinger*, she was overwhelmed and burst into tears. She had not thought that it could really happen.

Shortly after the election, she met the man whom she had first known as Joseph Cardinal Ratzinger and who was now called Benedict XVI. He said to her: "This was God's will." And he asked her to continue in his service.

She brought the new Pope's belongings from his apartment to the papal rooms, often on foot, just a few yards down the street, then through Saint Anne's Gate. On the evening after his solemn inauguration as Pope, she made supper for her close friends Georg Ratzinger and his housekeeper, Agnes Heindl: fresh strawberries, pasta, steak with artichokes, and red and white wine. Agnes Heindl says: "The table was beautifully laid out. Frau Stampa is intelligent, kind, and warm-hearted. She takes care of everything. She is a blessing for the Holy Father."

Professor Ingrid Stampa was the confidante who organized the day-to-day life of the Cardinal. She discussed appointments with his chauffeur before he got into his official blue Mercedes (with the number plate SCV-00338), which he had bought second-hand; now, he has to travel in an armor-plated car. When the Pope's bodyguard, Camillo Cibin (81), is present, she cooks pasta and fish. At the supper table, she talks about everything with Benedict XVI in their shared mother tongue.

Ingrid Stampa now has a new responsibility. She heads one of the departments in the Secretariate of State.

The Pope's guardian angel: Camillo Cibin (81) is the "Director of Security Services and Protection against Catastrophes" in the Vatican. He has been one of the papal bodyguards for forty-two years. The secret of his fitness: he eats the Mediterranean diet (pasta with fish or tomato sauce every day, one glass of red wine, three quarts of water).

The guardians of Catholic doctrine
meet behind these heavy doors.
Joseph Cardinal Ratzinger in
1999, on his way to a meeting in
the offices of Congregation for the
Doctrine of the Faith.

He Brings Us the Spirit of Joy in the Faith

By HANS-JOCHEN JASCHKE

Watchdog of the faith", "Grand Inquisitor": malicious (or perhaps merely ignorant) critics have given Benedict XVI these and similar labels. The name Peter means "rock". A Pope is not supposed to collapse or disintegrate. And it is easy to understand why modern people can find this difficult to accept.

"The Church is not something we can 'make'." I have often heard the Cardinal say these words. Clever management, tricks, and inventiveness are out of keeping with the nature of the Church. Ratzinger believes that we must perceive the Church in her own specific inner nature. She is a spiritual reality, a present we all receive from our parents, from reliable persons whom we love, and ultimately from God. We must take good care of such a present.

It would be disgraceful if people were to lose their delight in God's good gift through our fault. The new Pope is well aware that he is not the "maker" of the Church. He is always united to Jesus Christ and to the totality of the Bible and the great Christian tradition of all the ages. He can be confident that this gift will never become obsolete. He—and all of us—must rediscover it and hand it on to others with imagination and with vigor.

The Auxiliary Bishop of Hamburg, Jaschke, explains what Benedict XVI really stands for.

We have unhappy memories of the Grand Inquisitors. Their desire was to preserve the purity of the faith, but many official and unofficial little inquisitors rushed to help them in such a way that the light of faith no longer shone in human hearts. Pope John Paul II and Cardinal Ratzinger have publicly confessed the terrible guilt incurred by those who were intolerant and violent in God's name. This confession remains valid.

On the other hand, as the new Pope sees it, not everything in the Church can be negotiable. The faith has a form, indeed, an unambiguous form. We must be able to perceive that which necessarily remains reliable and valid for all times and persons.

The Two Great Concerns of the New Pope

First, faith must not dissolve. In our hearts, it is completely private, but it must retain the form given it by the Bible and the creeds.

Secondly, faith and reason need one another. Faith can give wings to reason, helping it to maintain a genuinely human sense of proportion. It is also true that reason casts a bright light on faith, helping to overcome any false one-sidedness. Reason brings faith into dialogue with men.

Reforms?

I am sure that Benedict XVI possesses the spirit of joy in the faith, a delight in that

Although considered by some to have been a modernizer as a young man, Joseph Cardinal Ratzinger has always carefully balanced tradition and doctrinal orthodoxy with openness and a respect for persons while engaging contemporary currents of thought.

Pope Benedict XVI sits between Vatican Radio journalists Emanuela Campanile (*left*) and Luca Collodi during a live broadcast in the "Nuova Regia 3" studio, at the Vatican Radio studios, on March 3, 2006. The visit was scheduled to mark the 75th anniversary of Vatican Radio, which broadcasts in forty languages around the world.

which is distinctively Christian, and that young people will find this a positive invitation. He is free of suspicion, timidity, or petty-mindedness. The new Pope is certainly aware of the problems of our time, such as abortion, contraception, or the position of women. These are problems that directly challenge people today. At the same time, the Pope knows that the Church may not condemn anyone. She addresses everyone with the assurance of God's love. She condemns no one.

But may one declare as a *norm* what many people de facto do—out of weakness, in distress, or under pressure? Abortion always remains the killing of an innocent human life. We must ensure that fewer women are put in such a position of distress. We must promote a culture of life in our world. This is one of the great concerns of the new Pope.

Benedict XVI emphasizes that sexuality is not a "thing". If it becomes a means to an end, it inflicts lasting damage. The correct use of sexuality, which includes the question of contraception, demands a personal responsibility with regard both to oneself and to one's spouse. The Church must warn against cheap solutions. She must protect men and women when such solutions are enforced on them by the state.

At the same time, the Church must respectfully realize the distress and the limitations of individuals in their existential situations. Benedict XVI argues that women must experience their total equality in the Church and that Christians must unite in the struggle against all discrimination, including that against women. His predecessor, Pope John Paul II, had already spoken of the need for an active and responsible presence of women in every field of the Church's activity.

In keeping with the Catholic tradition, the Pope recognizes the priesthood as a role for men. But he knows that this must not lead to an image of the Church as a "man's Church", that is, as an organization dominated by men. Here, we must all listen very attentively to the Holy Spirit.

We know that the new Pope is a prudent man who weighs well the decisions he makes. When we consider all the problems that exist, we can be sure that his sense of humor and his sometimes mischievous smile are good gifts for his ministry as builder of bridges to men, in whose hearts God wants to live.

Friends of God

By PETER SEEWALD

We will now speak of a friendship between two servants of God, a friendship where stimulating discussions played an important role. They were bound together by the bond of the faith.

John Paul II and Benedict XVI, the old Pope and the new, were companions on earth until they were separated by death. Before the coffin of John Paul II, Joseph Cardinal Ratzinger found words to describe the path they had traveled together: "He wanted to give of himself unreservedly, to the very last moment, for Christ and thus also for us."

In 1968, Joseph Ratzinger published his benchmark work *Introduction to Christianity*. In vigorous and eloquent terms, he demanded conservative reforms and a reflection on the faith. When he read this book, a young bishop in Krakow felt he had found a companion in the faith. Karol Cardinal Wojtyla, who was later elected Pope John Paul II, was attracted by the intellectual acuteness of the Bavarian.

They met at the Synod in 1977 and in 1978 and resolved that Germans and Poles should now walk more clearly on "the path toward each other" after all the painful years of the war and of hostility. They spoke the same language—the language with which they wanted to lead the Church into the future.

Ratzinger says: "I was initially attracted by his uncomplicated human directness and openness and by the warmth he radiated. One felt: this is a man of God."

The cross of faith, which they carried together for more than two decades. During the liturgy of the Passion on Good Friday 2004, Joseph Cardinal Ratzinger holds out the crucifix for Pope John Paul II, weakened by ill health, to kiss.

In October 1978, Karol Wojtyla was elected Pope, and one of the men he envisaged for a high office in the Vatican was Joseph Cardinal Ratzinger. A Vatican observer described the two men at that period as "intelligent reformers and conciliatory personalities".

The Pope offered Ratzinger the position of Prefect of the Congregation for the Doctrine of the Faith, in order to steer this world in the correct direction—the direction of the truth. But Ratzinger hesitated: "I put forward the arguments against my accepting this post, and he said that we should reflect further on this question."

In 1981, after the attack on John Paul II, the two men met again, "and he thought that he would not change his mind. I replied that I felt myself so much a theologian that I would like to continue to have the right to publish private works of my own, and I did not know if this was compatible with the new position. But it turned out that others before me had done so, and he said: 'No, that is not a problem, we can do that.' "

Joseph Cardinal Ratzinger accepted. He assumed the heavy burden of this new office and stood (so to speak) at the steering wheel of the Catholic Church: "Naturally, we have always discussed very important theological questions together. In that sense, I have naturally contributed to the doctrinal teaching of the Pope."

The Pope and his Cardinal became a very active team: the passionate actor and the brilliant thinker. The Pope's encyclicals bear the imprint of Ratzinger's desire to maintain Christian values, and he charged Ratzinger and his collaborators to produce a new catechism. The Pope praised the work: "When one reads the *Catechism of the Catholic Church*, one can grasp the marvelous unity of the mystery of God."

In August 2000, Ratzinger published the document *Dominus Iesus* on the uniqueness of the Christian faith. The Pope vigorously defended his guardian of the faith against worldwide accusations that this document contradicted the spirit of ecumenism. There were also divergences of opinion between the two churchmen: "It is natural that we can correct each other when we exchange information", says Ratzinger. "For example, we can say: This is correct, or this is wrong, or we need more information on this point." But whenever Ratzinger's strictness provoked opposition on the part of young believers, the Pope's mild gestures of

Brothers in spirit, companions in the faith, the old Pope and the new Pope. Here, Pope John Paul II and Joseph Cardinal Ratzinger once again celebrate the Easter ceremonies together.

reconciliation soothed the conflicts. They may not always have had the same opinion, but they complemented each other along their common path.

On his seventy-fifth birthday, as is customary in the Vatican, Joseph Ratzinger asked the Pope to accept his resignation from all his offices; but the Pope firmly declined, indicating publicly that he wished to keep the Prefect at his side. In this way, just three years before his death, John Paul II laid the unfinished tasks and his inheritance in the hands of the man from Bavaria.

Habemus papam!

By PETER SEEWALD

Joseph Aloysius Ratzinger was born on Holy Saturday, and in Holy Week, seventy-eight years later, he set out on the path that was to lead to his appearance on the balcony of Saint Peter's as Pope Benedict XVI.

Shortly before Easter of 2005, Ratzinger wrote the meditations that would be read at the stations of the Way of the Cross on Good Friday. In clear and vigorous language, he castigated the vacillating faith of so many people and spoke of a "purification" of the Church.

On the evening of Holy Saturday, he celebrated the Easter Vigil, and in view of the fact that the Pope was dying, many of the faithful looked at this Cardinal who radiated so much strength, firmness of will, and conviction. We heard the word *papabile*—a man who could be elected Pope.

Joseph Cardinal Ratzinger, a confidant of the Pope during his lifetime, was also one of his closest companions in the days and hours of his approaching death. The gravely ill Pope called him "my proven friend". And the Cardinal saw his own life as something that lay in the hands of his Creator: "My life is not composed of random chance incidents: rather, there is One who looks and thinks ahead of me and guides my life."

Finally, the day came when death separated the "team" of the Pope and his friend, the Cardinal and guardian of the faith. At 9:37 P.M. on April 2, the heart of the Holy Father stopped beating. Pope John Paul II was dead, and the scenario of mourning—whoever had written it—envisaged a leading role for Joseph Cardinal Ratzinger.

On April 8, he celebrated the Requiem Mass for John Paul II: "None of us can ever forget how on that last Easter Sunday of his life, the Holy Father, marked by suffering, came once more to the window of the apostolic palace.... We can be sure that our beloved Pope is standing today at the window of the Father's house, that he sees us and blesses us. Yes, bless us, Holy Father."

He celebrated the first Mass of the *novemdiales*, the nine days of official mourning that follow a Pope's death. He presided at the daily meetings of the cardinals, who had come to Rome from the four corners of the world and who all wanted to hear his views about the future of the Church. With his fluency in German, English, French, Italian, and Spanish, he impressed the cardinals in private conversations. In many audiences, he shared his ideas with his fellow cardinals who were to elect the new Pope in the conclave.

On April 16, he told his closest collaborators, as he celebrated his seventy-eighth birthday: "My voice is tired, because I have done nothing but speak all this last week." Msgr. Gerald Cadieres, an official in his Congregation, says: "His voice had become almost inaudible." There were still two days to go

> *"We can be sure that our beloved Pope is standing today at the window of the Father's house, that he sees us and blesses us"*

March 26, 2005
A "dress rehearsal" for
Joseph Cardinal Ratzing-
er. This evening, he
celebrates the Easter
Vigil in Saint Peter's
basilica. The photo-
graph shows him hold-
ing the Scriptures.
Ratzinger stands in for
Pope John Paul II, who
by now is gravely ill—
after a tracheotomy, he
can no longer speak.

FROM JOSEPH RATZINGER TO POPE BENEDICT XVI

During the Easter liturgy, Joseph Cardinal Ratzinger incenses the altar. In the Catholic liturgy, incense is regarded as a sign of the presence of God, of sacrifice, and of the ascending prayers of the believers.

before the conclave began, and the main daily newspapers in Rome were already calling Ratzinger the favorite to take over the Holy See. English bookmakers were quoting him in first place, at three to one. But the most important moment was still to come for Cardinal Ratzinger.

The 115 cardinal electors entered the Sistine Chapel to vote at 5:26 P.M. on April 18. That morning, in Saint Peter's basilica, Joseph Cardinal Ratzinger had preached a sermon that many considered an address in an electoral campaign. Even those who disagreed with this assessment saw the homily as an indication of the path that lay ahead. Here, he sketched the future of the Catholic Church: "We are moving toward a dictator-

ship of relativism that does not recognize anything as certain and that has as its ultimate standard one's own ego and one's own desires. However, we have a different standard: The Son of God, true man." These words echoed around the world. (See the text in the next section, pp. 122–25.)

After this sermon, one of Ratzinger's supporters said: "He certainly did not want the job. But as we looked at him, it seemed as if something in him had changed. It was almost as if he had already ascended to a new level."

The conclave began, but the first day brought no result: black smoke rose above the Sistine Chapel. It was only the second day that would bring a new Pope.

Entrance of the cardinals on Palm Sunday: Joseph Ratzinger and the Secretary of State, Cardinal Angelo Sodano, lead the procession with palm branches—an ancient church ritual at the beginning of Holy Week.

On April 19, the second and third ballots failed to reach the necessary two-thirds majority. In the third ballot, the German cardinal narrowly missed getting the seventy-seven votes needed.

The fourth ballot produced a majority. A few days later, Ratzinger described those moving moments: "When the counting of the votes made it clear that the ax would fall on my head, I thought: I had assumed that my life's work was completed, and I had looked forward to a few calm last years. At that moment, I prayed: 'Lord, don't do this to me!' But in this situation, the Lord clearly was not listening to me."

The Cardinal from Marktl am Inn received around ninety-five votes. A German had become Pope, and white smoke rose up. Joseph Cardinal Ratzinger chose the name Benedict XVI. The Chilean Cardinal Jorge Medina Estevez proclaims to Saint Peter's Square: "I announce to you a great joy. *Habemus papam*. We have a Pope."

At 6:49 P.M., Benedict XVI appeared in a white soutane on the balcony of Saint Peter's. As yet unaccustomed to all this, he spread out his arms and blessed the exultant faithful: "Dear Brothers and Sisters, after the great Pope John Paul II, the cardinals have elected me, a simple, humble worker in the vineyard of the Lord. I am consoled by the fact that the Lord knows how to work and to act even with inadequate instruments. And above all, I entrust myself to your prayers. With

Farewell: Archbishop Marini, Master of Ceremonies, bows before Pope John Paul II, whose body first lies in state in the Sala Clementina. Later, millions of pilgrims will pay their respects to him in Saint Peter's basilica.

CLEMENS VIII P M

CLEMENS VIII PONT MAX
AEDES A SIXTO V INCHOATAS
NE TANTI OPTIME DE SE
MERITI PONTIFIC
INSIGNIS AEDIFICATIO PERIRET
QVARTO SVI PONTIFICATVS
AN ABSOLVIT
SALVTIS M D XCV

115

The biggest funeral in history: over 400,000 in Saint Peter's Square and millions via television pray with Cardinal Ratzinger at the Mass for the deceased Pope John Paul II. The Gospel Book lies on his coffin.

the joy of the risen Lord and with confidence in his abiding help, we will move ahead. The Lord will help us, and Mary, his most holy Mother, will be at our side. I thank you."

Then the Pope began to pray and gave his first blessing *urbi et orbi*, to the city of Rome and to the whole world.

On the next day, the *Bild* newspaper carried the headline: *Wir sind Papst!* ("We Are Pope!"). Catholics everywhere in the world celebrated their new leader, but only his brother Georg was worried: "I was very surprised at the election, given the fact that he is so old. And his health is no longer so good. His heart! One oughtn't to lay such burdens on a man like him."

In his first Mass as Pope, Benedict XVI made it clear in whose spirit he understands his pontificate: "It seems I can feel his strong hand squeezing mine; I seem to see his smiling eyes and listen to his words, addressed to me especially at this moment: 'Do not be afraid!'"

On April 24, twenty-two days after the death of the old Pope, Benedict XVI was formally inaugurated as 264th successor of Saint Peter. Heads of state from around the world did him homage, including Federal Chancellor Gerhard Schröder and Federal President Horst Köhler from Germany.

Benedict XVI put the fisherman's ring on his right hand, and now he carried the shepherd's staff with which he would go ahead of the 1.1 billion Catholics of this world. The words of his sermon indicated the direction he would take: "Now, at this moment, weak servant of God that I am, I must assume this enormous task, which truly exceeds all human capacity.... But I am not alone.... How

"May the Lord be with you": at the close of the Requiem, Cardinal Ratzinger blesses the coffin in which Pope John Paul II lies.

FROM JOSEPH RATZINGER TO POPE BENEDICT XVI

"Lord, give me strength": Cardinal Ratzinger on April 16, during a Mass in Saint Peter's. He knows that he is viewed as one of the favorites at the conclave that is due to open in two days' time. Among the 115 cardinal electors, he is reckoned as *papabile*—capable of carrying out the difficult office of Pope.

often we wish that God would show himself stronger, that he would strike decisively, defeating evil and creating a better world. We suffer on account of God's patience. And yet, we need his patience.... Pray for me, that I may not flee for fear of the wolves."

Joseph Ratzinger
and the cardinals
pray at the grave
of John Paul II in
the crypt of Saint
Peter's basilica.

Lord, give us your blessing! On April 18, before the opening of the conclave, the 115 cardinals come together for a Mass in Saint Peter's at which Joseph Cardinal Ratzinger presides.

121

Against the Dictatorship of Relativism

Homily at Mass in Saint Peter's Basilica, April 18, 2005

By JOSEPH CARDINAL RATZINGER

At this hour of great responsibility, we hear with special consideration what the Lord says to us in his own words. From the three readings I would like to examine just a few passages that concern us directly at this time.

We hear with joy the news of a year of favor: Encountering Christ means encountering the mercy of God.

Let us dwell on only two points in the second reading. The first is the journey toward "the maturity of Christ", as the Italian text puts it, simplifying it a little. More precisely, according to the Greek text, we should speak of the "measure of the fullness of Christ", which we are called to reach in order to be true adults in the faith. We should not remain infants in the faith, in a state of immaturity. And what does it mean to be an infant in the faith? Saint Paul answers: It means "being tossed by waves and swept along by every wind of teaching arising from human trickery" (Eph 4:4). This description is very relevant today!

How many winds of doctrine we have known in recent decades, how many ideological currents, how many fashions of thinking.... The small boat of thought of many Christians has often been tossed about by these waves, thrown from one extreme to the other: from Marxism to liberalism, even to libertinism; from collectivism to radical individualism; from atheism to a vague re-

We have a different standard: the Son of God, true man

ligious mysticism; from agnosticism to syncretism, and so forth. Every day new sects are created, and what Saint Paul says about human trickery comes true, with a cunning that tries to draw people into error (cf. Eph 4:14).

Having a clear faith, based on the creed of the Church, is often labeled as fundamentalism, whereas relativism, which is letting oneself be tossed and swept along by every wind of teaching, looks like the only attitude acceptable to today's standards.

We are moving toward a dictatorship of relativism that does not recognize anything as certain and that has as its ultimate standard one's own ego and one's own desires.

However, we have a different standard: the Son of God, true man. He is the measure of true humanism. Being an "adult" means having a faith that does not follow the waves of today's fashions or the latest novelties. A faith that is deeply rooted in friendship with Christ is adult and mature. It is this friendship that opens us up to all that is good and gives us the knowledge to judge true from false and deceit from truth. We must become mature in this adult faith; we must guide the flock of Christ to this faith. And it is this faith—faith alone—that creates unity and is realized in love. On this theme, Saint Paul offers us some beautiful words. In contrast to the continual ups and downs of those who are like infants, tossed about by the waves, he says that we must

Hold fast to your faith! Joseph Cardinal Ratzinger during the Mass in Saint Peter's. Before the conclave, he appeals to all Catholics: "Being an 'adult' means having a faith that does not follow the waves of today's fashions."

FROM JOSEPH RATZINGER TO POPE BENEDICT XVI

"perform the truth in love". This is the basic formula of the Christian existence. In Christ, truth and love merge. Love without truth would be blind; truth without love would be like a "resounding gong or a clanging cymbal" (1 Cor 13:1)....

The second element of the Gospel reading to which I would like to refer is the teaching of Jesus on bearing fruit: "I chose you and appointed you to go and bear fruit and that your fruit should abide" (Jn 15:16). Here we see the dynamism of the apostle's Christian existence: "I chose you to go...."

We must be inspired by a holy restlessness: restlessness to bring to everyone the gift of faith, of friendship with Christ. In truth, the love and friendship of God have been given to us that they might also be shared with others. We have received the faith so that we might give it to others—we are priests meant to serve others. And we must bear a fruit that will abide. Everyone wants to leave a mark that lasts. But what lasts?

Money does not last, nor do buildings or books. After a certain amount of time, long or short, all these things pass away. The only

thing that lasts forever is the human soul, man created by God for eternity. Thus, the fruit that abides is what we have sown in the hearts of men: love, knowledge, a gesture that touches the heart; a word that opens the soul to the joy of the Lord. Let us then go to the Lord and beseech him to help us bear fruit—a fruit that abides. Only thus will the earth be transformed from a vale of tears into the garden of God....

Our ministry is a gift of God to men, in order to build up his Body—a new world. Let us live our ministry in this way, as Christ's gift to men! But at this time above all, we pray insistently to the Lord that after the great gift of Pope John Paul II, he may give us a new pastor after his own heart, a pastor who will lead us to the knowledge of Christ, to his love and to true joy. Amen.

The first day of the conclave begins with Mass in the packed basilica of Saint Peter's. At the altar stands Joseph Cardinal Ratzinger, at this point regarded as a favorite in the forthcoming election to the papacy.

125

FROM JOSEPH RATZINGER TO POPE BENEDICT XVI

April 19, 2005: White smoke ascends from the chimney of the Sistine Chapel—a new Pope has been elected. A dove flies up into the sky— a symbol of peace. At 6:06 P.M., the bell of Saint Peter's (*right*) begins to ring. The first peals cannot be heard because of the exultation of the crowd down on the Square—the world has a new Pope.

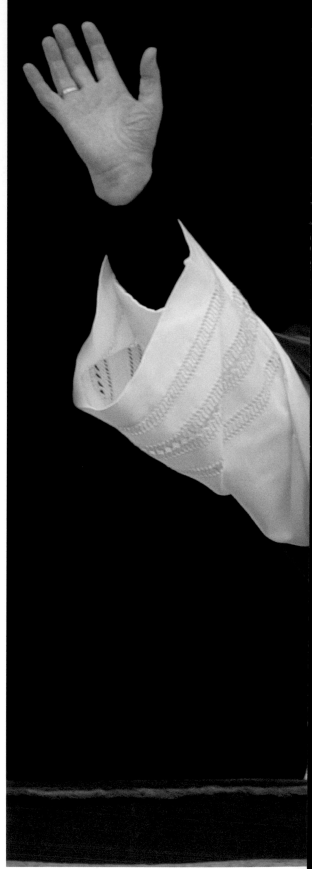

Habemus papam—we have a Pope! Benedict XVI appears for the first time on the loggia of Saint Peter's. On the tapestry: the coat of arms of John Paul II (1920–2005).

Welcome, Pope Benedict XVI!
The former Joseph Cardinal
Ratzinger enters the loggia
of Saint Peter's as the new
Pope and waves radiantly to
the faithful. He is the first
German on Saint Peter's throne
for 482 years.

"A simple and humble worker in the Lord's vineyard—I entrust myself to your prayers", says Benedict XVI in his first address as Pope. He speaks fluent Italian.

Benedict XVI gives his first blessing *urbi et orbi* (for the city of Rome and the world) as Pope. Tens of thousands in Saint Peter's Square cheer, while millions watch on live television.

131

How the New Pope Will Change the World

By PETER SEEWALD

Joseph Ratzinger became a scholar, a bishop, a guardian of the faith. And yet, he always had "this burning feeling that I was not living up to my vocation, to the idea that God had of me and of what I could and must give". Now, the theologian on the chair of Peter can accomplish what remains to be accomplished.

John Paul II gave the See of Peter a worldwide prestige that had not existed before. His successor now has the opportunity, not only to be applauded, but to be listened to. There were many negative clichés about Joseph Ratzinger, and he surprises people simply by being himself: cheerful, warm, and humble. As Benedict XVI, immediately after the conclave, he announced in brief terms the tenor of his mission: "One who believes is never alone. Do not be afraid of Christ! He takes nothing away, and he gives you everything."

Many of his opponents were like spinning tops, revolving around their own private theology, but Ratzinger was always in touch with the latest developments. When it was important to break open encrustations, he broke them open. When it was important to hold the faith and the Church together against the forces that would dissolve them, he held them together. As the Munich theologian Eugen Biser notes, the present Pope has always related his teaching to that of the saints and the Church Fathers, but with the aim of "making the Church dynamic and alive and giving her fresh impetus upon her path".

"One who believes is never alone. Do not be afraid of Christ! He takes nothing away, and he gives you everything", says the Pope

Benedict XVI is more than merely a steward of the inheritance from John Paul II. While bringing the seed sown by his predecessor to maturity, he will at the same time develop a style of his own. He has said that the task is to defend the claim to *truth* against the new idol of an arbitrariness that levels everything and against the "dictatorship of relativism".

His experiences under National Socialism taught him that the Church "is not helped in the slightest by mere institutional guarantees: there must be men who support the Church out of an innermost conviction." His choice of name—after Benedict, who renewed Europe—indicates that he sees as one of his priorities the rescue of a Western society that has lost its soul: "The debate about the definition of Europe has consequences for the whole of humanity."

Here are the main emphases of the new pontificate:

Concentration Instead of Excessive Action

According to Pope Benedict XVI, the real crisis of the Church is the lack of prayer and contemplation. We must return to the beginnings, that is, to the origin of the Church in the mystery of Christ. To bear witness means to live an authentic Christian life.

"Benedictus XVI"—the new Pope practices his signature. He wears a white skullcap of moiré silk, a soutane with thirty-three buttons, and the pectoral cross.

First audience in the Vatican: two nuns greet the new Pope.

Why Did He Choose the Name Benedict?

The name Benedict comes from the Latin *benedictus* (the "blessed man"). By choosing this name, Benedict XVI looks back to Saint Benedict of Nursia, the great religious founder and educator. His motto *ora et labora* ("pray and work!") and the Rule he wrote in Montecassino laid the foundations for a new start in Europe. Hundreds of thousands of his monks cultivated the soil of western Europe with agriculture, scholarship, and culture. Benedict is the patron saint of Europe. In Bavaria, the Pope's homeland, *terra benedicta* ("the blessed land") is a name

given to the regions made so fertile by the Benedictines.

At the same time, the German Pope looks back to his predecessor Benedict XV (Pope from 1914 to 1922).

He is remembered as "the Pope of peace" and as a great missionary. It is not surprising that Ratzinger, who has played such a prominent role in social debates for decades, should have chosen a name that recalls another man who got involved in politics.

Christians must get involved. It goes without saying that the Pope is called to plead for peace and reconciliation in a lacerated world. The name of the new Pope can be read as a prophecy of the mission he is to fulfill.

134

Reducing Institutional Power

The institutional power of the huge Churches in some countries is strangling them. "I fear that we may be so absorbed in our own structures that we forget that the goal of the Church is the realization of love of one's neighbor in the world." It has always been good for the Church to become small, humble, and loving: "The Church must part with her 'goods' in order to retain her 'good'."

Fulfilling the Work of the Council

Ratzinger has summed up the experience of the Council by saying that while "a leap forward" had been expected, there soon came a "process of decline". The Church cannot win over men by adapting to the world; all she will do thereby is to lose her own self. All the documents of the Council remain valid. True reform consists, not in a watering down of the faith, but in its radicalization.

Involvement in Society

From the very beginning, the faith has had the power to transform society. "Without a basis in Christian values," warns Ratzinger, "democracy cannot survive." The world "needs to be reminded of the ethics of the fathers, of that which made the civilized cultures great".

Ecumenism

Benedict XVI pointedly put on a pallium with red crosses during his official inauguration Mass. This style of pallium was last worn by a German Pope, Leo IX, before the great schism of 1054: a signal for the path to unity, especially with the Eastern Churches.

New Discovery of the Church and of Faith

The Christian faith gives answers and support, especially in a sick society that is increasingly marked by egoism and the lust for profit. We must rediscover the power, truth, and beauty that are contained in the mysteries of the faith. Without this dimension, man cannot develop fully: "As soon as we cease to honor God, man, too, loses his splendor."

The Eucharist and the Protection of Life

The heart of the Christian life and the source of our relationship to God is the celebration of the Holy Eucharist. Benedict XVI is not content simply to urge that "the liturgy be carried out correctly." He also demands the indivisible protection of that human life which is God's gift. Marriage, family, and children form a part of God's universal ordering. Without them, no society can survive. He warns that a catastrophe of unimaginable horror would ensue if man in his present creation were to be changed by genetic manipulation.

Mission

Relationship to God is neither a game nor a purely private matter. Without the values of the Christian religion, politics and society deprive themselves of one of their fundamental sources. The question of religion has become acute throughout the world today, not only in times of floods and other natural disasters. In Germany, the marginalization of Christianity leads to a religious state of emergency, with grave consequences for the identity and also for the cultural and economic level of the country. The Pope from Germany, with all the aura and the weight of his high office, can now perhaps bring about some change in the land where the Reformation was born.

Many Catholics happily interpret the World Youth Day of August 2005 as a signal. But as soon as Benedict XVI was elected, his books became bestsellers overnight, making possible a "catechesis" that no one would have thought possible before. At the same time, people began to discuss the values and the identity of the German nation, with a new interest in the relationship between faith and culture, faith and the environment, and, not least, faith and the economy, since the religious decline of a people is usually followed by a decline in its intellectual and economic productivity. The pontificate of Benedict XVI allows us to envisage the "new spring of the

Viva il Papa tedesco!—Long live the German Pope! Joseph Ratzinger meets the crowds. He is traveling from Saint Peter's Square to his former apartment in the Piazza della Città Leonina.

New clothing, new apartments. Pope Benedict XVI and his closest collaborators visit his private rooms in the Apostolic Palace. In the background we see his housekeeper, Professor Ingrid Stampa.

Immediately after the conclave, Benedict XVI wears the papal white soutane. Three different sizes were prepared before the election.

human spirit" that his predecessor prophesied as a reality!

Young people experience Christianity anew as the basis of their understanding of the world and of human life, as a viable, meditative, and reflective religion that helps them discover meaning and healing—and that creates solidarity with the sufferings and the sufferers of this world.

Ratzinger says that Christ's main wish was "an exodus from what people had gotten used to". This sounds very modern. Eugen Biser holds that this Pope has in fact brought about something utterly unexpected, "namely, the rediscovery of the Church", because "he has consistently related Christianity back to the figure of Jesus."

One day before his solemn inauguration, Benedict XVI receives bishops who work in the Vatican offices. They kiss his ring as a sign of fidelity.

The first press conference of the new Holy Father. In the audience hall of the Vatican, Benedict XVI speaks to more than 5,000 journalists. He thanks them for their sensitive coverage of the last months of John Paul II's life and asks them to make their talents available to the service of society.

The "simple worker in the Lord's vineyard" becomes his Vicar on earth. During his solemn inaugural Mass, Benedict XVI incenses the altar on which the fisherman's ring lies.

Shortly after this, he puts the ring on his right hand. This golden ring bears the image of Saint Peter and the name of the new Pope.

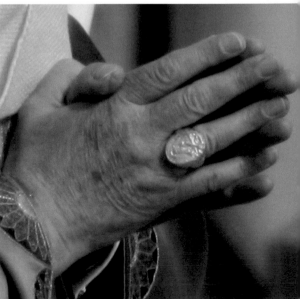

A ritual act of humility before God and the eyes of the world, at his inaugural Mass, the new Pope Benedict XVI ascends to and kisses the altar. On his right lies Sacred Scripture and the fisherman's ring, a sign of his authority as the Successor of Saint Peter, the first Pope.

He sends his greeting to the four corners of the earth. With his right hand, now bearing the fisherman's ring, Benedict XVI waves to the faithful. On his shoulders, he wears the pallium, a band of sheep's wool (8.5 feet in length) signifying the yoke of Christ and the shepherd's mission as guardian of Christ's flock.

She kneels in faith: a nun kisses the Holy Father's ring.

Benedict XVI steps carefully at the beginning of his new life, at his first public Mass as the 264th successor of Saint Peter. In his hand, he carries the cross and has red leather shoes on his feet—like the emperors in ancient Rome.

The first journey in the "pope-mobile", without protective bullet-proof glass. After his inaugural Mass, Benedict XVI travels through the exultant crowds.

The days of grief are past: the crowds cheer their new Pope. Hundreds of cameras click as Benedict meets the crowds.

In their enthusiasm, people touch his garments and hold out a child for him to bless.

149

Queen Sofia of Spain kisses the ring of Benedict XVI. Her husband, King Juan Carlos, stands behind her.

King Carl Gustav of Sweden pays his respects to the new Holy Father and shakes his hand.

Only a few days after the death of his father, Prince Albert of Monaco pays homage to the Pope.

The head of the Church and the Federal President of Germany: Horst Köhler and his wife, Eva, greet the Pope.

The Prime Minister of Bavaria, Edmund Stoiber, and his wife, Karin, pay their homage to the Holy Father.

The German federal chancellor bows before the German Pope. Gerhard Schröder's wife, Doris, wears the traditional black veil and kneels before Benedict XVI.

I Am Not Alone!

Homily at the Mass of Inauguration, Sunday, April 24, 2005

By POPE BENEDICT XVI

How alone we all felt after the passing of John Paul II—the Pope who for over twenty-six years had been our shepherd and guide on our journey through life! He crossed the threshold of the next life, entering into the mystery of God. But he did not take this step alone. Those who believe are never alone—neither in life nor in death. . . .

And now, at this moment, weak servant of God that I am, I must assume this enormous task, which truly exceeds all human capacity. . . . All of you, my dear friends, have just invoked the entire host of Saints, represented by some of the great names in the history of God's dealings with mankind. In this way, I too can say with renewed conviction: I am not alone. I do not have to carry alone what in truth I could never carry alone. All the Saints of God are there to protect me, to sustain me and to carry me. And your prayers, my dear friends, your indulgence, your love, your faith and your hope accompany me. . . .

Yes, the Church is alive—this is the wonderful experience of these days. During those sad days of the Pope's illness and death, it became wonderfully evident to us that the Church is alive. And the Church is young. She holds within herself the future of the world and therefore shows each of us the way towards the future. The Church is alive, and we are seeing it: we are experiencing the joy

"The Church is alive—she is alive because Christ is alive, because he is truly risen"

that the Risen Lord promised his followers. The Church is alive—she is alive because Christ is alive, because he is truly risen. . . .

Dear friends! At this moment there is no need for me to present a programme of governance. I was able to give an indication of what I see as my task in my Message of Wednesday 20 April, and there will be other opportunities to do so. My real programme of governance is not to do my own will, not to pursue my own ideas, but to listen, together with the whole Church, to the word and the will of the Lord, to be guided by him, so that he himself will lead the Church at this hour of our history. Instead of putting forward a programme, I should simply like to comment on the two liturgical symbols which represent the inauguration of the Petrine Ministry. . . .

The first symbol is the Pallium, woven in pure wool, which will be placed on my shoulders. This ancient sign, which the Bishops of Rome have worn since the fourth century, may be considered an image of the yoke of Christ, which the Bishop of this City, the Servant of the Servants of God, takes upon his shoulders. . . .

The symbolism of the Pallium is even more concrete: the lamb's wool is meant to represent the lost, sick or weak sheep which the shepherd places on his shoulders and carries to the waters of life. For the Fathers of the Church, the parable of the lost sheep, which the shepherd seeks in the desert, was an image

"Yes, the Church is alive—this is the wonderful experience of these days." Benedict XVI preaches in the presence of hundreds of thousands of the Catholic faithful during his inaugural Mass.

153

of the mystery of Christ and the Church. The human race—every one of us—is the sheep lost in the desert which no longer knows the way....

What the Pallium indicates first and foremost is that we are all carried by Christ. But at the same time it invites us to carry one another. Hence the Pallium becomes a symbol of the shepherd's mission, of which the Second Reading and the Gospel speak. The pastor must be inspired by Christ's holy zeal: for him, it is not a matter of indifference that so many people are living in the desert. And there are so many kinds of deserts. There is the desert of poverty, the desert of hunger and thirst, the desert of abandonment, of loneliness, of destroyed love. There is the desert of God's darkness, the emptiness of souls no longer aware of their dignity or the goal of human life. The external deserts in the world are growing, because the internal deserts have become so vast. Therefore the earth's treasures no longer serve to build God's garden for all to live in, but they have been made to serve the powers of exploitation and destruction.... It is not power, but love that redeems us! This is God's sign: he himself is love. How often we wish that God would show himself stronger, that he would strike decisively, defeating evil and creating a better world.

All ideologies of power justify themselves in exactly this way, they justify the destruction of whatever would stand in the way of progress and the liberation of humanity. We suffer on account of God's patience. And yet, we need his patience. God, who became a lamb, tells us that the world is saved by the Crucified One, not by those who crucified him. The world is redeemed by the patience of God. It is destroyed by the impatience of man....

The second symbol used in today's liturgy to express the inauguration of the Petrine Ministry is the presentation of the fisherman's ring. Peter's call to be a shepherd, which we heard in the Gospel, comes after the account of a miraculous catch of fish: after a night in which the disciples had let down their nets without success, they see the Risen Lord on the shore. He tells them to let down their nets once more, and the nets become so full that they can hardly pull them in; 153 large fish.... And then came the conferral of his mission: "Do not be afraid. Henceforth you will be catching men"....

Both the image of the shepherd and that of the fisherman issue an explicit call to unity. "I have other sheep that are not of this fold; I must lead them too, and they will heed my voice. So there shall be one flock, one shepherd" (*Jn* 10:16); these are the words of Jesus at the end of his discourse on the Good Shepherd. And the account of the 153 large fish ends with the joyful statement: "although there were so many, the net was not torn" (*Jn* 21:11).

Alas, beloved Lord, with sorrow we must now acknowledge that it has been torn! But no—we must not be sad! Let us rejoice because of your promise, which does not disappoint, and let us do all we can to pursue the path towards the unity you have promised. Let us remember it in our prayer to the Lord, as we plead with him: Yes, Lord, remember your promise. Grant that we may be one flock and one shepherd! Do not allow your net to be torn, help us to be servants of unity....

And so, today, with great strength and great conviction, on the basis of long personal experience of life, I say to you, dear young people: Do not be afraid of Christ! He takes nothing away, and he gives you everything. When we give ourselves to him, we receive a hundredfold in return. Yes, open, open wide the doors to Christ—and you will find true life. Amen.

Full of pride, but also concern: Georg Ratzinger watches his brother, Pope Benedict XVI, on television.

The seven German Popes before Benedict XVI

 ▶ **Gregory V** (996–999). He became Pope thanks to the support of Emperor Otto III.

 ▶ **Clement II** (1046–1047). He was poisoned and died on October 9, 1047. His tomb is in the cathedral of Bamberg.

 ▶ **Damasus II** (1048). He died of a malarial illness in Palestrina on August 9, 1048.

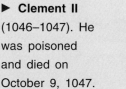 ▶ **Leo IX** (1049–1054). He fought against simony and lay investiture.

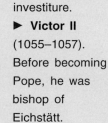 ▶ **Victor II** (1055–1057). Before becoming Pope, he was bishop of Eichstätt.

 ▶ **Stephen (IX) X** (1057–1058). He was committed to the reform of the Church.

 ▶ **Adrian VI** (1522–1523). He attempted in vain to have the Reformer Martin Luther declared an outlaw at the Imperial Parliament in Regensburg.

Throw open the doors to Christ....
Professor Ingrid Stampa, the housekeeper of Benedict XVI, opens the
shutters of the private papal apartment in the Apostolic Palace on
April 30.

Benedict XVI greets the faithful from the window of his apartment: "I appear for the first time at this window, which countless people in the world have come to know, thanks to my beloved predecessor."

Pontiff of Love

By PETER SEEWALD

What kind of a Pope is this, whose first encyclical speaks of love?

Let us recall what people were saying: A "Grand Inquisitor" as the Vicar of Christ? An old man longing for rest as the head of the biggest global organization in history? John Paul II was a giant of the faith. It seemed impossible that any successor could take up his mantle and carry on his inheritance. One year later, everything looks different: the predecessor carried the Church over the threshold, and the successor—without any break in continuity—is building a bridge strong enough to take the Church into the third millennium.

The new Pope could not be more radical. He wants to waken a tired community of faith out of its lethargy. He cries out: "Christianity is full of undiscovered dimensions." A year after he began his pontificate, we can say that he has truly astonished us:

"Christianity is full of undiscovered dimensions"

1. The Beginning

Benedict XVI began cautiously, almost as if he were not the Vicar of Christ but the Vicar of Wojtyla, to whom he referred continually. Almost overnight, with the death of John Paul II, a generation of believers came into public view. They had hardly been noticed until then. They were young, cheerful, and pious, an invaluable help at the start of the "new spring of the human spirit" that Karol Wojtyla had predicted.

The new Pope unleashed a new enthusiasm: millions began studying his writings. Thanks to his gifts as a teacher, he engages in a continuous catechesis that is penetrating, authentic, and, at the same time, provocative.

2. Acceptance

The Italians were the first to be caught up in the enthusiasm: they called the Pope from Germany a genius full of wisdom and humor. Even today, up to 60,000 persons stream to hear him speak in Saint Peter's Square, more than ever before. It has become fashionable among intellectuals to speak positively about Ratzinger, and even his former critics have suddenly found themselves in agreement with him.

Are there then two Ratzingers? Yes and no! Those who knew the former cardinal always found him a kind and helpful man. For decades, he accepted without complaint the burden of watching over the faith, but now another dimension has entered his life. Benedict's secret: "Suffering is the path of transformation, and without suffering nothing changes."

3. His Style

Ratzinger is different. He does not wear his heart on his sleeve, and he seems fragile when he appears in public. Now, when he apparently possesses supreme power, he seems more

The Holy Father in the course of his daily work: Benedict XVI in his private library on May 23, 2005, at the end of a meeting.

powerless than ever—and it is precisely this that makes him so impressive and convincing.

First, he quietly abolished the custom of kissing the Pope's hand. Then the tiara, the symbol of the worldly power of his throne, disappeared from his coat of arms. Wojtyla had become accustomed to speaking of himself in the singular. After the "I", Ratzinger reintroduced the papal "We"—but this was in order to make episcopal collegiality, not his own person, the center of attention.

4. The Central Themes of the Pontificate

Immediately after his election, he declared his intention to pursue "an inner renewal" that would point the Church in the right direction—"against every temptation to accommodation, watering down, and opportunism". As Pope, he has worked in a concentrated and consistent manner. His task is to ensure "that the Word of God is preserved in its fullness and is heard in all its purity". The basic lines are clear:

Christ is "the Lord of all creation and of all history"

Jesus is the Son of God and Redeemer of the world. Benedict insists that the roots of Christianity must come to light anew. Christ is "the Lord of all creation and of all history". Accordingly, "every other truth is only a fragment of the truth that he is and to which he leads." It is striking to see how this theologian, who emphasizes Jesus so strongly, becomes more "Marian": the best way to get to know Jesus is through Mary.

The Eucharist and the liturgy: For Catholics, the presence of Christ in the Mass is the greatest mystery in the world. Jesus bequeathed it to us, and it is absolutely essential to us. The Pope affirms that we can experience the whole power of Jesus only if our starting point is the Mass.

Ecumenism: Every day, each Christian is called to account for what he has done for ecumenism. The goal is "the reestablishing of complete and visible unity".

Religious dialogue: The Holy Father's first official act was to send a letter to the Jewish community in Rome. At the World Youth Day in Cologne, Benedict said that he wanted to continue "with full vigor" on "the path of improving our relationship and friendship with the Jewish people".

5. The High Points

The Pope also sees the Church as the community of values that opposes the decadence of society on behalf of the coming generation. The World Youth Day gave great impetus to this movement.

The World Synod of Bishops in October 2005 had an exemplary character. The length of the synod was reduced, and at the same time it was made more of a forum for debate.

In his first encyclical, *Deus caritas est* ("God is love"), Benedict is not afraid to tackle the subject of sex. But he does not speak only of contraception and celibacy. Rather, he speaks of the necessary liberation of eros from arbitrariness; it is not something to be bought and sold. With this "invitation", he wishes to show "the human quality of faith, man's 'yes' to his own bodiliness, which has been created by God".

The second part of the text is about the transformation of eros into "agape", sacrifice for others, *caritas*. He castigates the horrors of an unbridled capitalism and the misuse of religion: if God's essence is love, then no one is permitted to summon others to hatred and violence in the name of God.

6. Looking Ahead

"God is not indifferent to human history", the Pope emphasizes. "It is his wish to realize with us and for us a plan of unity and peace."

After his election, his great call is to clear the way for Jesus Christ. After so many fruitless discussions and a paralyzing self-absorption,

ELECTED POPE

On May 26, Benedict XVI celebrates Mass on the feast of Corpus Christi in Saint John Lateran in Rome, one of the oldest churches in the city. It is the Pope's own cathedral in his function as Bishop of Rome.

Benedict XVI with his private secretary, Msgr. Georg Gänswein.

The Pope receives the Swiss guards before the new recruits take their oath.

the Church must now come to learn the mystery of the Gospel anew and to present Christ in all his mystical greatness.

It is obvious that the Pope is becoming not only a dialogue partner but also some-

one who gives meaning to a world that has become spiritually empty, the prophet of a just and free society. His first encyclical ends with a poetical core statement. "Love is the light—and in the end, the only light—that

can always illuminate a world grown dim and give us the courage needed to keep living and working. Love is possible, and we are able to practice it because we are created in the image of God" (no. 39).

On May 15, the Pope ordains twenty-one new priests in Saint Peter's basilica. They will exercise the ministry in various parish churches in Rome.

On May 19, the film *Karol—A Man Who Became Pope*, about the life of John Paul II, has its premiere in the Vatican. This film also shows how Karol Wojtyla helped Jews under the Nazi occupation of Poland. On this occasion, Benedict XVI speaks of his own memories of the Nazi period. He says that we should never forget the genocide of the Jews and that we must never permit such crimes to be committed anew.

FROM JOSEPH RATZINGER TO POPE BENEDICT XVI

The Pope's first holiday: like his predecessor, Benedict XVI spends his summer holiday in Les Combes in the Aosta valley (*large photograph*). After a meeting with priests, he is greeted by a group of children (*below*) and then visits a museum dedicated to John Paul II (*bottom left*).

After a general audience in Saint Peter's Square on June 22, the Pope kisses a baby.

Pilgrimage in Rome: Benedict XVI in the "popemobile" May 26 (with an altar and the monstrance) en route to basilica of Saint Mary Major, the largest of the forty churches in Rome dedicated to the Mother of God.

The Pope leaves the office of President Ciampi of Italy, after visiting him on June 24.

167

"God's Revolution"

The World Youth Day in Cologne

By PETER SEEWALD

Before the World Youth Day, critics such as Eugen Drewermann dismissed it as "mere fun" and a cheap "entertainment industry". In reality, it was the largest and surely the most beautiful manifestation of the Christian faith that has ever taken place in Germany. At its close, the World Youth Day in Cologne brought together 1.1 million people from 200 nations—a complex event full of dynamism for the future. "Young people are not looking for a Church that artificially pretends to be young", said the Pope. "They are looking for a Church that is young in the Spirit." Many elements in the message of those days will take time to develop and bear fruit, but the signals for a new start were obvious. "God is different!" cried Benedict. Like the Magi who followed the star, people today must learn to become "men of truth, of justice, of kindness, of forgiveness, of compassion".

The young people called out in chorus: "Be-ne-dett-o!" In four days, he had twenty-one appointments. He took part in an ecumenical encounter; he received politicians; he prayed at the shrine of the three Wise Men, the most precious reliquary in all the Christian world. The successor of Peter recalled the victims of the fascist terror in the Cologne synagogue: "Shalom, peace be with you! Before God, all men have the same dignity, irrespective of the people, the culture, or the religion to which they belong."

The Pope said he was "happy to be among young people. I would love to drive in the 'popemobile' along every single row of you." Sex, contraception, celibacy? Old hat. Instead, the Pontiff turned the World Youth Day into a vital catechesis, a powerful school of faith. He urged the young to practice eucharistic adoration, which is the path to union with God. Keep Sunday holy. Discover the Eucharist: only one who learns to love the Mass will be able to find the nourishment of its infinite power. It is Jesus who can bring about a kind of "splitting of the atom" within us: an "explosion of goodness, which overcomes evil". For "it is not ideologies that save the world. The real revolution consists only in a radical turning to God, who is the criterion of justice and who is eternal love. —And what could save us, if not love?"

Reporters noted an "overwhelming feeling of togetherness and peace". Bishop Wolfgang Huber, the president of the Council of Protestant Churches in Germany, said that they too felt "especially moved". The World Youth Day gave great prominence above all to the humility of those who took part—and to the charism of the Holy Father. The Italian press commented: Now we are seeing a Pope who speaks of a loving and merciful God and of the Church as a "place of tenderness".

> *"No one is unwanted. Everyone is loved. Everyone is needed."*
> Benedict XVI at the World Youth Day in Cologne

Benedict XVI's first journey abroad as Pope brings him to Germany. On August 18, he arrives at the Cologne/Bonn airport.

Peace be with you!
On August 18, Pope Benedict XVI greets the visitors to the World Youth Day in Cologne from a ship on the Rhine.

Enthusiasm and cries of joy on the bank of the Rhine: young people standing up to their hips in the water in order to be near the Pope as he passes by on his ship.

The Holy Father blesses Victor, a child suffering from cancer.

Benedict XVI waves to the pilgrims outside Cologne cathedral.

171

On August 19, the Pope greets Bishop Wolfgang Huber, chairman of the Council of the Evangelical Church in Germany, at an ecumenical encounter.

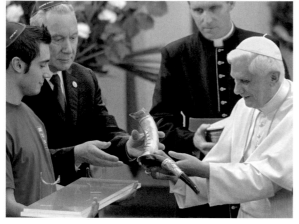

In Cologne, members of the Jewish community present the Pope with a *shofar*, the ceremonial ram's horn that is a symbol of reconciliation.

... And he meets leading representatives of the German Muslims.

"We have come to worship him" (Mt 2:2). On August 20 the Pope greeted around 700,000 pilgrims with Evening Prayer at the 20th World Youth Day at Marienfeld in Germany.

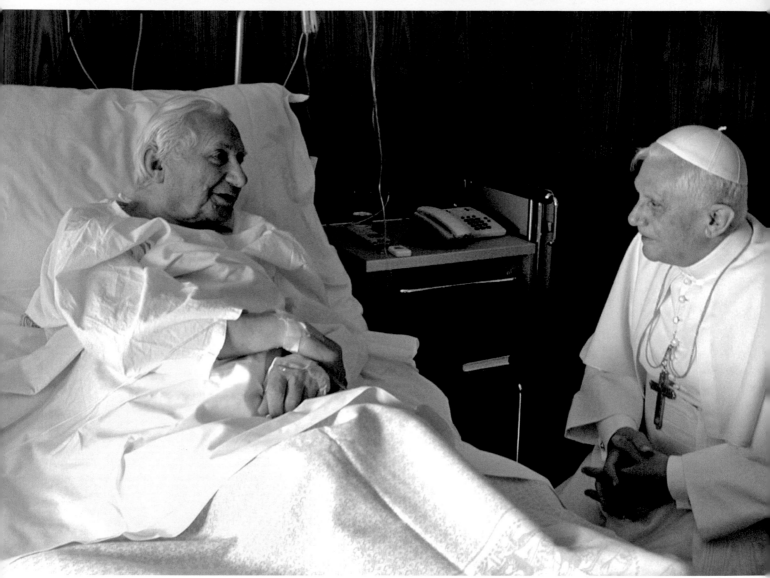

Benedict at the bedside of his brother, Georg Ratzinger, who had a heart operation in the Gemelli Clinic in Rome.

On September 14, the Pope blesses a new statue for Saint Peter's basilica for the first time. It depicts the founder of the Catholic lay movement Opus Dei, Saint Josemaria Escrivá (canonized in 2002).

Applause! Benedict after a concert by the Munich Philharmonic Orchestra in the Vatican (which was subsidized by the BILD newspaper).

A song from his native land: the Regensburg "Domspatzen" choir sings for the Pope in the Sistine Chapel. His brother, Georg Ratzinger, directed this choir from 1964 to 1994.

Benedict XVI thanks Christian Thielemann (56), the director of the Munich Philharmonic Orchestra, for the concert.

At the beginning of October, in Saint Peter's basilica, Benedict XVI inaugurates the first Synod of Bishops during his pontificate.

Bavarians in Rome: Benedict XVI and German soccer legend Franz Beckenbauer, "Der Kaiser", after the general audience on October 26 (with the pennant of World Cup soccer) . . .

. . . and with Edmund Stoiber, prime minister of Bavaria, on November Stoiber presents the Pope with a statue of our Lady made of Nymphenburg porcelain.

GOD'S SERVANT

Every Wednesday, the Pope blesses the faithful at his general audience in Saint Peter's Square—as here, on October 19, 2005.

FROM JOSEPH RATZINGER TO POPE BENEDICT XVI

On November 10, Benedict XVI receives President Talabani of Iraq (to the left of the Pope) and his delegation in the private papal library.

The Pope, who was himself a fireman in his seminary days, receives a new fire engine for the Vatican fire brigade.

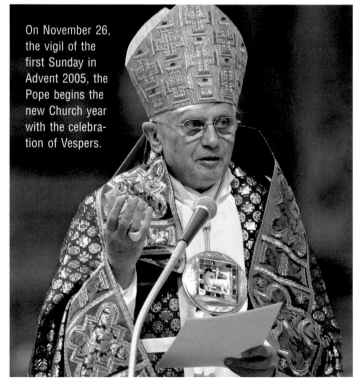

On November 26, the vigil of the first Sunday in Advent 2005, the Pope begins the new Church year with the celebration of Vespers.

In November, Benedict receives guests from
Africa, representatives of the Tuareg people
who have come for the beatification of
Charles de Foucauld (1858–1916), who
lived as a missionary among their people.

FROM JOSEPH RATZINGER TO POPE BENEDICT XVI

At the general audience on December 21, Benedict XVI protects himself against the cold with the camauro, the traditional papal headgear.

Four days after Christmas, thousands of the faithful greet the Pope enthusiastically in Saint Peter's Square. His red velvet cap featured in many photographs.

A present: on December 14, Kai Diekmann, chief editor of BILD newspaper, presents the "Golden Bible" of BILD and *Weltbild* to the Pope after the general audience.

A Christmas message for the whole world: on December 24, the Holy Father celebrates Midnight Mass, which is televised live in seventy countries.

A candle on Candlemas Day (February 2). This feast, forty days after the birth of Christ, concludes the cycle of Christmas feasts in the Church calendar.

182

On January 22, 2006, the five-hundredth anniversary of the Swiss Guards is marked by a Mass in the Sistine Chapel.

On January 25, 2006, in his study, Benedict XVI puts his signature to his eagerly awaited first encyclical, *Deus caritas est* (*God Is Love*).

After the Angelus prayer, during which Benedict XVI prays for the people killed when a flat roof caved in under the weight of snow in Poland, a white dove flies upward.

Biography

1927: Joseph Aloysius Ratzinger, the son of the policeman Joseph Ratzinger and Maria Ratzinger, is born on April 16 in Marktl am Inn in Bavaria. It is Holy Saturday, and the newborn child is baptized with the first blessed water of Easter.

1929: The family moves to Tittmoning on the Salzach river.

1932: Ratzinger's family moves first to Aschau am Inn, and later to Hufschlag. Joseph Ratzinger begins his primary schooling.

1941: Ratzinger is enrolled at the diocesan minor seminary of Saint Michael in Traunstein. The seminary is forced to enroll him in the Hitler Youth.

1943/1944: Joseph Ratzinger now attends the Elector Maximilian High School in Munich, where only a reduced education is provided, because of the war. Ratzinger graduates from this high school. He is made an anti-aircraft auxiliary in Munich and must defend the BMW factory against attacks from the air. In 1944, he is enlisted for compulsory work in the service of the Reich in Burgenland and is enlisted in the infantry

toward the end of the year. Ratzinger deserts and is taken prisoner by the Americans.

1945: In June, Ratzinger is released from the prisoner-of-war camp.

1946: Joseph Ratzinger studies philosophy and Catholic theology at the Philosophical and Theological Academy in Freising and at the University of Munich. In 1951, he takes his final examinations.

1951: Ratzinger is licensed to teach at the University of Munich and in Freising. In June, he and his brother, Georg, are ordained to the priesthood. Joseph Ratzinger is appointed to a summer supply in the parish of Saint Martin in Moosbach (Munich).

1951/1952: Curate of the Precious Blood parish in Munich.

1952: Ratzinger is appointed to lecture in the archdiocesan seminary in Freising.

1953: Ratzinger takes his doctorate with a dissertation on "People and House of God in Augustine's Doctrine of the Church".

What Does His Coat of Arms Mean?

Benedict XVI chose a coat of arms with a shield divided into three fields, which has scarcely changed from the coat of arms he bore as a bishop, with its motto: "Co-Workers of the Truth". On the left is the mysterious "Moor of Freising", who has featured on the coats of arms of the bishops in the archdiocese of Munich and Freising for the last thousand years. It was in Freising that Ratzinger was ordained to the priesthood in 1951. The bear of Saint

Corbinian with a pack-saddle, "God's beast of burden", symbolizes the burdens of ecclesiastical office. The third element is a shell, symbolizing man's pilgrimage on earth. Augustine borrows this image to express the impossibility of fully understanding the greatness of God, the immense ocean of his wisdom and mercy. One might as well try to bail out the entire sea with one single shell! Editor Peter Seewald comments on the mystery of the papal coat of

arms: "The Moor stands for Ratzinger. The Moor, whom many people fear because he is so different, so inconvenient, so provocative. And the Moor who has not yet done his full duty, who must bring his work to fulfillment." Benedict XVI is the first Pope in the modern period to dispense in his heraldic device with the tiara, the crown that symbolizes secular power.

1954: Ratzinger is appointed lecturer in dogmatics and fundamental theology at the Philosophical and Theological Academy in Freising.

1957: Ratzinger completes his professorial dissertation under the fundamental theologian Gottlieb Söhngen on the theme of "Saint Bonaventure's Theology of History".

1958: Ratzinger is appointed to an associate professorship at the Academy in Freising.

1959: Ratzinger's father dies. He becomes professor of dogmatics at the University of Bonn.

1962: Joseph Cardinal Frings, Archbishop of Cologne, appoints the young Professor Ratzinger his adviser. Ratzinger writes for the Cardinal the speeches that will subsequently leave their mark on the Second Vatican Council. He is appointed an official conciliar theologian and a member of the Commission for Doctrine of the German Bishops and of the International Pontifical Theological Commission in Rome.

1963: Ratzinger's mother, Maria, dies. He is appointed professor of dogmatics and the history of dogma at the University of Münster.

1966: Professor of dogmatics and the history of dogma at the University of Tübingen.

1969: Professor of dogmatics and the history of dogma at the University of Regensburg.

1977: Pope Paul VI appoints Ratzinger Archbishop of Munich and Freising, in succession to the deceased Julius Cardinal Döpfner. In June of the same year, the Pope creates him cardinal. Initially, he retains an honorary professorship at the University of Regensburg. He is awarded the Bavarian Order of Merit.

1978: As cardinal, Joseph Ratzinger takes part in the two conclaves. In October, the Polish Cardinal Karol Wojtyla is elected Pope John Paul II.

1981: Pope John Paul II appoints Cardinal Ratzinger Prefect of the Congregation for the Doctrine of the Faith; Ratzinger leaves Munich for Rome, where he acquires Vatican citizenship. He is also appointed President of the Pontifical Biblical Commission and the International Theological Commission.

1982: There is an acute conflict between Ratzinger and Latin American liberation theology, whose spokesman, Leonardo Boff, claims that the Church has misunderstood the historical Jesus. When Ratzinger asks Boff to keep silent on this subject for a year, he acquires the reputation of a "hardliner".

1984: Ratzinger is appointed a member of the Congregation for the Causes of the Saints.

1986: Pope John Paul II sets up a commission to produce a new *Catechism of the Catholic Church*. Ratzinger is its president and spends about five years on this task. Chancellor Helmut Kohl awards Ratzinger the Great Cross of Merit of the Federal Republic of Germany with Star and Sash.

1991: Ratzinger's sister, Maria, dies. At the plenary assembly of the college of cardinals in Rome, Ratzinger attacks the laws permitting abortion in the developed countries, calling these "a culture of death". He condemns the feminism that does not set women free but helps enslave them. In September, he suffers a slight stroke and must spend a month in hospital.

1993: Pope John Paul II appoints Ratzinger to the rank of cardinal bishop, with the suburbicarian titular see of Velletri-Segni.

1997: Marktl am Inn makes Joseph Ratzinger an honorary citizen.

1998: Ratzinger is appointed Commander of the French Legion of Honor.

1999: Ratzinger is one of the signatories to the "Joint Declaration on Justification" between the Catholic Church and the Lutheran World Federation.

2000: Ratzinger, as Prefect of the Congregation for the Doctrine of the Faith, publishes the controversial document *Dominus Iesus*, which emphasizes the unique nature of the Catholic Church vis-à-vis all other Christian bodies.

2002: In April, Joseph Cardinal Ratzinger asks the Pope to accept his resignation for reasons of health, but John Paul II declines. Ratzinger is elected dean of the college of cardinals in succession to Bernardin Cardinal Gantin.

2005: On April 2, Pope John Paul II dies at the age of eighty-four. Joseph Cardinal Ratzinger is the principal celebrant at his funeral Mass and then leads the conclave for the election of the 264th successor of Peter in the Holy See. On April 19, an overwhelming majority of the 115 cardinal electors choose him as the new Pope. He takes the name Benedict XVI. On April 24, in the course of a Mass celebrated on Saint Peter's Square, his new ministry is inaugurated.

2006: On January 25, Benedict XVI publishes his first papal Encyclical, *God Is Love* (*Deus Caritas est*), which immediately meets with general approval throughout the world.

Bibliography

Studying in the name of the Lord: In 1982, Joseph Ratzinger came to Rome with 2,000 books. He has written more than 135 theological works.

Twenty-two Important Books by Joseph Cardinal Ratzinger

Called to Communion: Understanding the Church Today. Translated by Adrian Walker. San Francisco: Ignatius Press, 1996.

Christianity and the Crisis of Cultures. Translated by Brian McNeil, C.R.V. San Francisco: Ignatius Press, 2006.

The Feast of Faith: Approaches to a Theology of the Liturgy. Translated by Graham Harrison. San Francisco: Ignatius Press, 1986.

God and the World: Believing and Living in Our Time. A Conversation with Peter Seewald. Translated by Henry Taylor. San Francisco: Ignatius Press, 2002.

God Is Near Us: The Eucharist, the Heart of Life. Translated by Henry Taylor. San Francisco: Ignatius Press, 2001.

Images of Hope: Meditations on Major Feasts. Translated by John Rock and Graham Harrison. San Francisco: Ignatius Press, 2006.

Introduction to Christianity. Translated by J. R. Foster. With a new preface, translated by Michael J. Miller. San Francisco: Ignatius Press and Communio Books, 2004.

Many Religions—One Covenant: Israel, the Church, and the World. Translated by Graham Harrison. San Francisco: Ignatius Press, 1999.

Mary: The Church at the Source, by Joseph Cardinal Ratzinger and Hans Urs von Balthasar. Translated by Adrian Walker. San Francisco: Ignatius Press and Communio Books, 2005.

Milestones: Memoirs 1927–1977. Translated by Erasmo Leiva-Merikakis. San Francisco: Ignatius Press, 1998.

The Nature and Mission of Theology: Essays to Orient Theology in Today's Debates. Translated by Adrian Walker. San Francisco: Ignatius Press, 1995.

A New Song for the Lord: Faith in Christ and Liturgy Today. Translated by Martha M. Matesich. New York: Crossroad, 1997.

On the Way to Jesus Christ. Translated by Michael J. Miller. San Francisco: Ignatius Press, 2005.

Pilgrim Fellowship of Faith: The Church as Communion. Translated by Henry Taylor. San Francisco: Ignatius Press, 2005.

Principles of Catholic Theology: Building Stones for a Fundamental Theology. Translated by Sister Mary Frances McCarthy, S.N.D. San Francisco: Ignatius Press, 1987.

The Ratzinger Report: An Exclusive Interview on the State of the Church. An interview with Vittorio Messori. Translated by Salvator Atanasio and Graham Harrison. San Francisco: Ignatius Press, 1985.

Salt of the Earth: Christianity and the Catholic Church at the End of the Millennium. An Interview with Peter Seewald. Translated by Adrian Walker. San Francisco: Ignatius Press, 1997.

The Spirit of the Liturgy. Translated by John Saward. San Francisco: Ignatius Press, 2000.

Truth and Tolerance: Christian Belief and World Religions. Translated by Henry Taylor. San Francisco: Ignatius Press, 2004.

Turning Point for Europe? The Church in the Modern Word—Assessment and Forecast. Translated by Brian NcNeil, C.R.V. San Francisco: Ignatius Press, 1994.

Values in a Time of Upheaval: Meeting the Challenges of the Future. Translated by Brian McNeil. San Francisco: Ignatius Press and New York: Crossroad, 2006.

What It Means to Be a Christian: Three Sermons. Translated by Henry Taylor. San Francisco: Ignatius Press, 2006.

Photographs

The German publisher has endeavored as far as possible to identify those who have the rights to the photographs. Where an oversight means that the sources are not indicated, or given erroneously, we ask for pardon. Those who own the rights are asked to get in touch with the publisher, and this list will be corrected in subsequent editions. All photographs are copyrighted by their owners.

Abbreviations: a = above; c = center; b = below; l = left; r = right.

Front cover: Giancarlo Giuliani/CPP, **Inside front cover:** Getty Images/HO, **5:** BILD, **6:** Marco Delogu/Contrasto/Agentur Focus, **7:** Sammy Minkoff, **8/9:** AP/Diether Endlicher, **10:** AP/Domenico Stinellis, **11:** Edizione Paoline, **12/13:** Corbis/Stringer, **14:** AP/Pier Paolo Cito, **15:** AP/Pier Paolo Cito, **16/17:** Unimedia International/Marucci, **18/19:** dpa/Kay Nietfeld, **20:** AP/Gregorio Borgia, **21:** dpa/Archdiocese of Munich and Freising, **22/23:** Corbis/Kai Pfaffenbach, **24:** KNA-Bild, **25:** Robert Piffer, **26/27:** Corbis/Jerry Lampen, **28:** Lapresse/Angeli, **29:** Contrasto/Agentur Focus, **30/31:** Gamma/Sestini Agency, **32/33:** Corbis/L'Osservatore Romano/Arturo Mari, **34:** Gnoni-Press/Masi, **35:** Private, **37:** Getty Images/HO, **38:** KNA-Bild, **39:** SIPA/Facelly, **40/41:** Getty Images/HO, **40b:** Getty Images/HO, **43a:** SIPA/Facelly, **43bl:** SIPA/Facelly, **43br:** Corbis/Stringer, **45:** Corbis/Stringer, **47:** KNA-Bild, **48/49:** Argum/Falk Heller, **51:** Private (first published in J. Cardinal Ratzinger, *Aus meinem Leben:*, DVA 1998), **53al:** AP/HO, **53ar:** BILD/Peter Mueller, **53b:** Corbis/Darrin Zammit Lupi, **54/55:** Private, **57:** KNA-Bild, **59:** dpa/private, **60/61:** Corbis/Stringer, **63:** AFP/ddp/Reproduction Timm Schamberger, **65:** Corbis/Stringer, **66:** Corbis/Stringer, **69:** photothek/Ute Grabowsky, **70/71:** dpa/Wirginings, **72c:** KNA-Bild, **72/73:** dpa/Ludwig Hamberger, **74:** KNA-Bild, **75:** BILD-archive photograph, **76/77:** dpa, **78:** KNA-Bild, **79:** SV-Bilderdienst/F. Neuwirth, **80a:** Ullstein/Hampel, **80b:** BILD-archive photograph, **81:** Interfoto/amw, **82a:** dpa/Gerhard Rauchwetter, **82bl:** dpa, **82br:** AP/Claus Hampel, **83:** dpa, **85:** SIPA/Galazka, **86:** KNA-Bild, **87:** actionpress/Azimut Multimedia, **88/89:** Gamma/Sestini Agency, **90:** KNA-Bild, **91:** Sammy Minkoff, **92:** SV-Bilderdienst/K.-H. Egginger, **93:** actionpress/Eva Schmidt, **94/95:** Gamma/Sestini Agency, **97al:** dpa/Oliver Berg, **97cr:** AP/L'Osservatore Romano, **97bl:** Queen/Reflex, **97br:** Corbis/Alessia Pierdomenico, **98/99:** Gamma/Vandeville Eric, **100/101:** Contrasto/Agentur Focus, **102:** Ullstein/Sawatzki, **103:** dpa/EPA, **104:** Vatican Pool/CPP, **106/107:** Getty Images/Danilo Schiavella, **108/109:** Gamma/Giuliani Alessia/CNS, **111:** SIPA/Galazka, **112:** Grzegorz Galazka, **113:** Getty Images/Vincenzo Pinto, **114/115:** Getty Images/Massimo Sambucetti, **116:** AP/Massimo Sambucetti, **117:** Corbis/Alessandro Bianchi, **118al:** ROPI/Picciarella/Eidon, **118bl:** dpa/EPA/Maurizio Brambatti, **118/119:** Corbis/Mari, **120/121:** Corbis/Gianni Giansanti/Immaginazione, **123:** Iaif/James Hill, **124:** Agentur Focus/Fotografia Felici/Grazia Neri, **125:** Getty Images/L'Osservatore Romano Pool, **126al:** Getty Images/Andreas Solaro, **126ar:** Angeli/Venturelli, **126b:** Marco Merlini/Lapresse/

PHOTOGRAPHS